115610

SO-ATO-270

The Battle for the Gospel

The Battle for the Gospel

The Bible and the Reformation 1444-1589

Marvin W. Anderson

Baker Book House
Grand Rapids, Michigan

Copyright 1978 by

Baker Book House Company

ISBN: 0-8010-0121-8

Library of Congress Catalog Card Number: 77-91119

Printed in the United States of America

Illustrations on pp. 20, 77, 84, 131 by permission of the Syndics of Cambridge University Library

.609cbl4
tb

L.I.F.E. College Library
1100 Glendale Blvd.
Los Angeles, Calif. 90026

To My Father
WALTER R. ANDERSON
Faithful Minister of the
GOSPEL

032983

LIST OF ILLUSTRATIONS

Contents

Preface

In his preface to *Patterns of Reformation,* Gordon Rupp writes:

> It is part of the glorious liberty of the children of wisdom that everyman may be a freeman of the world of learning, free to go where he will, to ponder whatever seems to him profitable or intriguing, to pause, to take up a subject and put it down again, and if he likes, to turn back and return to his first love. Long may that liberty continue!

Twenty-five years ago as a university freshman I listened with gusto to lectures on Valla and Valdés, Luther and Loyola, Calvin and Castellio. In seminary days E. Harris Harbison's *The Christian Scholar in the Age of the Reformation* inspired me to serious study of these biblical scholars. Graduate study in Europe and a sabbatical leave at Cambridge University with Professor Rupp guided me down many a fascinating bypath of Reformation Europe. After several side trips I am happy to return to a synoptic view of the Bible and the Reformation.

Marvin Anderson

Introduction

We must recall how the medieval church loved Scripture; it adored biblical narrative in story, sermon, and art. (Scripture permeates St. Benedict's sixth-century Rule.) Church audiences were often amused by biblical plays in everyday language, such as this report about the animals which Noah's family brought into the ark:

> *Shem.* Sir, here are lions Libyan.
>   Horses, mares, ox, and swine,
>   Goats, calves, sheep, and kine,
>   Here thou may see.
> *Ham.* Camels, asses, men may find,
>   Buck, doe, hart, and hind;
>   Beasts of every sort and kind,
>   Here I think there be.
> *Japhet.* Here are cats and dogs as well.
>   Otter, fox, fullmart you smell.
>   Hares, by their hopping you can tell.
>   And cows for to eat.
> *Noah's Wife.* And here are bears and wolves, a set.
>   Apes and owls and marmoset,
>   Weasels, squirrels, and ferret:
>   Here they eat their meat.
> *Shem's Wife.* Yet more beasts are in this house!
>   Here are cats, all most jocose,
>   Here's a rat, and here a mouse,
>   All standing high together.
>   And here are fowls, all in their turn,
>   Hearns and cranes, and loud bittern,
>   Swans and peacocks—in the stern,
>   To ride the coming weather.
> *Japhet's Wife.* Here are cocks, and kites, and crows,

> Rooks and ravens . . . many rows.
> Cuckoos, curlews, . . . whoso knows
>   Each one in his kind.
> And here are doves, and ducks, and drakes,
> And redshanks running through your lakes,
> Every fowl that sleeps and wakes,
>   In this ship many may find.

The animals proved much easier to bring aboard than Noah's wife herself, who was unwilling to enter the ship without her friends. Just in time, her sons picked her up bodily and shoved her up the gangplank.[1] Such biblical narratives may have been popular in the late medieval period, but serious Scripture study was another matter.

The *People's Bible* is also evidence of the level of medieval devotion to Scripture. It drew attention to the seven deadly sins and the seven godly virtues based on Isaiah 11:2f. The *Biblia Pauperum* of the fourteenth century contained thirty-four scenes drawn from the New Testament, beginning with the Annunciation and ending with the descent of the Holy Ghost. Each of these was set between illustrations of two Old Testament incidents—complete with four prophets and appropriate texts. These manuscripts supplied intellectually poor preachers with sermons and the people with pictures.

A third example of late medieval interest in biblical interpretation is the *Ordinary Gloss* drawn up under Anselm of Laon. This "standard commentary" patched together patristic remarks, monastic piety, and mystical insights on the page to surround a small section of the biblical text. The gloss to Genesis 6:14-16 interprets Noah's orders to build the Ark:

> Noah built the ark of incorruptible timbers as Christ built the Church with men who were going to live for eternity, and the Church floats above the waters of tribulation just as the Ark floats on the waves. The ark is made up of squared timbers; so the Church, made up of saints whose life is firm and ready for all good works, resembles squared timbers that stand firm at every point. The timbers are fixed together with pitch inside and outside, so that this compact unity may symbolize charitable patience, the virtue which prevents the Church from being so dis-

---

1. Roland Bainton, *The Church of Our Fathers* (Philadelphia: Westminster Press, 1950), p. 111.

turbed by those within or without as to depart from brotherly concord. For pitch is the hottest and strongest form of glue and it symbolizes the fervour of charity and its strength for holding together a society which endures all things. Now the fact that the ark is six times as long as it is broad and ten times as long as it is deep presents an exact likeness with the human body in which Christ was made manifest. . . . Then, the broad expanse of fifty cubits symbolizes the manner in which the heart expands under the influence of that love which the Holy Ghost inspires, as the apostle said: "the love of God hath been shed forth in our hearts". For it was on the fiftieth day after the Resurrection that Christ sent forth the Holy Spirit which expanded the hearts of the faithful. Now a length of three hundred cubits amounts to six times fifty, and in the same way the whole extent of time falls into six ages, in which Christ was proclaimed without ceasing: in the fifth he is the subject of prophecy, while in the sixth he is openly proclaimed in the Gospel.[2]

Beryl Smalley's *The Bible in the Middle Ages* describes the disappointing trend of Scripture interpretation among late medieval scholars. They did not possess the allegiance to Hebrew scholarship that characterized their predecessors (men like Nicholas of Lyre), and their brand of intepretation—a predisposition for the spiritual—required them to ignore the careful work of their forerunners. Smalley concludes: "It meant throwing overboard the fruits of some hard, honest thinking."[3]

The Renaissance, however, meant a new situation for biblical study. The sixteenth century opened men's eyes to serious reflection on the text of Scripture. The Bible, as we have seen, was familiar to the medieval church. The Reformers did not find the Bible; rather, they claimed to discover the gospel.

"God, open the King of England's eyes" cried William Tyndale as Henry's agents betrayed and burned him in Belgium that sunny August day in 1538. But they could as soon close the Bible as end the sunshine. Five years later, Scotland permitted folk to read what Tyndale gave his

2. R.L.P. Milburn, "The 'People's Bible': Artists and Commentators," in *The Cambridge History of the Bible,* ed. G.W.H. Lampe, vol. 2, *The West from The Fathers to the Reformation* (Cambridge: At the University Press, 1969) 2:295.

3. Beryl Smalley, "The Bible in the Middle Ages," in *The Church's Use of the Bible Past and Present,* ed. D.E. Nineham (London: S.P.C.K., 1963), pp. 70–71.

life to see in print—the Bible in vernacular dress. John Knox, the Scottish Reformer, exulted:

> Then might the Bible have been seen lying upon almost every gentleman's table. . . . They would chop their familiars on the cheek with it and say, "This has laid hidden under my bed foot these ten years." Others would glory, "O! how often have I . . . stolen from my wife at midnight to read upon it."[4]

Some cared then as much for the Word of God as zealous Marxists do now for theories of history and economics. Let us listen to three faithful witnesses from sixteenth century Europe. The Dutch humanist Erasmus wrote:

> I would that even the lowliest women read the Gospels and the Pauline Epistles. And I would that they were translated into all languages so that they could be read and understood not only by Scots and Irish but also by Turks and Sarecens. . . . Would that, as a result, the farmer sing some portion of them at the plow, the weaver hum some parts of them to the movement of his shuttle, the traveller lighten the weariness of the journey with stories of this kind! Let all the conversations of every Christian be drawn from this source.[5]

Thomas Cranmer, Archbishop of Canterbury (martyred in 1556), contributed a preface for the second edition of the 1539 Great Bible:

> In the Scriptures be the fat pastures of the soul; therein is no venomous meat, no unwholesome thing; they be the very dainty and pure feeding. He that is ignorant, shall find there what he should learn. He that is a perverse sinner, shall there find his damnation to make him to tremble for fear. He that laboureth to serve God, shall find there his glory, and the promissions of eternal life, exhorting him more diligently to labour. Herein may princes learn how to govern their subjects; subjects, obedience, love and dread to their princes: husbands, how they should behave them unto their wives; how to educate their children and servants: and contrary, the wives, children, and servants may know their duty to their husbands, parents and masters. Here

---

4. John Knox, *Works* cited in Rupp, "The Bible in the Age of the Reformation," in *The Church's Use Of The Bible,* p. 86.

5. Carl S. Meyer, "Erasmus on the Study of Scriptures," *Concordia Theological Monthly* 40 (1969):742.

may all manner of persons, . . . of what estate or condition soever they be . . . learn all things what they ought to believe, what they ought to do, and what they should not do, as well concerning Almighty God, as also concerning themselves and all other. Briefly, to the reading of the Scripture none can be enemy, but that either be so sick that they love not to hear of any medicine, or else that be so ignorant that they know not Scripture to be the most healthful medicine.[6]

And Martin Luther penned his spiritual testimony two days before his death in 1546. It sums up his lifetime of gospel discovery:

No one can understand Vergil in his shepherd poems and peasant songs, if he has not himself been a shepherd or a peasant for five years. Cicero's letters cannot be understood, I contend, by anyone who has not been seasoned for twenty years in political affairs. No one should think that he has tasted Holy Scripture adequately if he has not, with the prophets, led congregations for a century. So tremendous is the miracle of John the Baptist, of Christ, of the apostles. . . . Bow reverently over his tracks. We are beggars. That is true.[7]

Each of these men acted upon his longing to reach the people with Scripture. Erasmus provided sixteenth-century travelers with the biblical stories to lighten the weariness of their trek. Cranmer tried for six years in England to apply the medicine of Scripture to heal the sickness of spirit and sadness of soul. And Luther's reverence before the miracle of Holy Scripture reminded all that before God they were indeed beggars. That is true!

The Bible and the Reformation could fill volumes of careful study by teams of experts on printing, humanism, and political upheaval in that volatile century. The story of biblical study in the Reformation is like a fine painting: sometimes a Bruegel-like masterpiece crammed with details and clusters of peasants; at other times a Cranach portrait of a stout Reformer or intense scholar. On occasion the scenario shifts to one of Albrecht Dürer's woodcuts, such as *Melancholy,* or *Knight,*

---

6. A.G. Dickens and Dorothy Carr, *The Reformation in England to the Accession of Elizabeth I* (London: Edward Arnold Publishers Ltd., 1967), p. 113.

7. Willem Jan Kooiman, *Luther and the Bible* (Philadelphia: Muhlenberg Press, 1961), pp. 238–39.

Death and the Devil. Often Dürer's four horsemen of *The Apocalypse*
thunder past to remind us that we visit a century of famine, pestilence,
war, and death.

One pattern for our subject might indeed derive from the sixteenth-
century Nürnburg artist Dürer; not with melancholy, but with the consolation of the gospel. As one turns to Dürer's painting of the *Four
Apostles* he sees in the two panels John opening the Word to Peter, and
Mark holding a copy of Scripture. Paul, sword in hand, faces Mark.
Dürer affixed Scripture to each of the panels and introduced the four
texts with a phrase that means "Accordingly these four excellent men
heed the warning of Peter, John, Paul and Mark."

One way to approach the study of the Bible and the Reformation
would be to use these four Scripture warnings chosen by Dürer to open
up a discussion of internal problems in Protestantism. When II Peter 2:1
speaks of false teachers and prophets who secretly bring in false heresies, our minds turn to Luther's *Sermon Against the Heavenly Prophets,*
his rejection of the Zwichau prophets such as Thomas Müntzer, and the
issues surfacing in the 1520s in Wittenberg. When I John 4 instructs one
to test false prophets for their views of the incarnation, we think of
Calvin and the ugly scene in which Michael Servetus was burned at
Geneva in 1553 while saying, "Jesus, Son of the eternal God, pray for
me." Servetus could not pray to Jesus, eternal Son of God. In the
sixteenth century, men died for their interpretation of such phrases.
When II Timothy 3 urges political obedience to rulers, we are reminded
of the Peasant's War in Germany, and the French Protestant resistance
theory after the St. Bartholomew massacre of August 1572. When
Dürer's fourth passage, Mark 12:38, warns against scribes who parade
their piety in public, we remember the English Cardinal Wolsey's proud
accumulation of church offices, or Pope Julius II, who was the object
of Erasmus' biting satire. Heresy, Christology, political rebellion, and
piety survey four segments of Reformation uses of Scripture.

A second pattern emerges as we view the circumstances surrounding
the first printed English Bible, published by Miles Coverdale in 1535.
Queen Anne Boleyn commanded that an English Bible be laid on her
desk so that all might read it when they would. She urged Henry VIII
to set up an English Bible in every parish church. Thomas Cromwell
issued a series of injunctions in 1536 which ran as follows:

> Every parson . . . shall . . . provide a book of the whole bible,
> both in Latin and also in English . . . and comfort, exhort and
> admonish every man to read the same as the very word of God
> and the spiritual food of man's soul. . . . [8]

These injunctions were printed in mid-July; but alas, the queen had
been arrested on May 2 and executed on the 19th. Consequently, the
injunctions were never enforced. Anne's support and Cromwell's injunc-
tion meant that the *Coverdale Bible* had come very close to being the
first vernacular Bible set up in the English parish churches. However, it
fared no better than Henry's queen; she lost her head in the Tower of
London.

This first complete English Bible (1535) describes sixteenth-century
biblical concerns on its title page. Across the top are drawings of Adam
and Eve of Genesis 2 with the text, "In what daye so euer thou eatest
therof, thau shalt dye." Adjacent is the second Adam of Matthew:
"This is my deare sonne, in whom I delyte, heare him. Matth. 17." Two
other pairs of drawings emerge along the left and right borders. The
first contrasts the Ten Commandments with the gospel. The texts read
alternately, "These are the lavves, that thou shalt laye before them"
and "Go youre vvaye into all the vvorlde, and preach the Gospel."
After Moses and Christ, the next pair of drawings shows Esra reading
the Scripture (I Esdras 9) and Peter preaching in Acts 8:2. The bottom
illustration is of the king taking the Bible from mitred bishops, flanked
on the left panel by King David and on the right by St. Paul. David,
harp in hand, sings from Psalm 118, "How svveet are thy vvordes," and
Paul says he is "not ashamed of the gospell of Christ, for it is the povver
of God," as in Romans 1.

Much of Protestant biblical concern can be found in these panels and
the three Scriptures centered under the title. The first Adam dead in sin
is flanked by the Second Adam, the strong resurrection Son of God.
Law and gospel present the relation of Old Covenant to the New, while
the reading of Scripture is balanced by its preaching. King David sang
and St. Paul spoke as bold examples for English royalty to support the
Bible. II Thessalonians 3, Colossians 3, and Joshua 1 complete the title
page. They urge that "the worde of God maie have fre passage" and

---

8. J.F. Mozley, *Coverdale And His Bibles* (London: Lutterworth Press, 1953), pp.
120–21.

that "the worde of Christ dwell in you plenteously in all wysdome." A quote from Joshua 1 completes this trilogy, instructing, "Let not the boke of this lawe departe out of thy mouth."

Queens and commoners, kings and popes, secretaries and scholars now had enacted before their very eyes that word of sin and grace, law and gospel, and the mighty deeds of salvation history. Coverdale's title page of 1535 depicts a fascination for the divine/human nature of God's Word, written in Scripture and incarnated in Christ. What did all this mean for the early sixteenth century? Which illustration shall we choose to sense the vitality of the Pauline Renaissance? Shall we select the first and second Adam Christology in the Latin commentaries on Romans 5:12-21 and I Corinthians 15:22, 34-39, or choose law and gospel as the theological essence of Protestantism? Shall we again explore the vernacular translations and volumes of printed sermons as the vehicles of reform? Each would foster a trek through the decades of biblical study in the sixteenth century.

Many patterns emerge as we probe our subject. Dürer's four texts form one path; Coverdale's title page leads to another. One could also explore the Bible in country after country, explaining translations, local liturgies and prominent reformers. A fourth avenue might reveal the kind of problems which biblical study illumined in the sixteenth century: as men debated politics and piety or heresy and Christology, sharp dissent arose over selected passages such as John 1, Romans 13, Matthew 13, John 6, and Romans 9—11.

I suggest rather that we enter our subject by turning to the concerns of four types of reformers; namely, the humanist interest in the study of the Holy Writ, the Wittenberg clashes over Word and Spirit, the Reformed concern for the clarity of Scripture, and the Catholic crisis over Scripture and tradition.

First of all appears the humanist concern for Greek, Hebrew and all that; second, the Luthern concern for order; third, the Reformed attitude toward the certainty of the Word and radical obedience to it, and finally, the issue of Scripture and tradition raised within Catholicism at Trent by certain Cardinals who read Scripture. When we take this approach and commence with persons who study Scripture, the local patterns of piety and passionately-held heresy soon emerge at every corner.

1 | Humanists and Holy Writ

COMMENTARY

Greek, Hebrew, and All That

Our story begins with a tale told by John Kessler in his *Sabbata*.

In 1522, Kessler and a companion traveled to Wittenberg to study Holy Scripture. On the way, the weary travelers stopped at the Black Bear Inn at Jena for the night. There they met a knight with red hood and a sword at his side; he was reading a book. The travelers asked, "Sir, can you tell us whether Dr. Martin Luther is in Wittenberg just now, or where else he may be?" The disguised Luther answered, "I know for certain that he is not in Wittenberg at this moment. But Philip Melanchthon is there and he teaches Greek and others teach Hebrew." Kessler relates that the knight "advised us strongly to study these two languages which were above all needful for the study of holy scripture. . . . And so we marveled at this knight who knew all about Philip and Erasmus, and about how useful it was to know Greek and Hebrew. . . . We thought this must be a very uncommon knight."

The conversation broke the ice, and Kessler's companion took the book from the stranger's hand and opened it. It was a Hebrew psalter. Kessler's comrade cried, "I'd have my little finger cut off if I might only learn this language!" To which Luther answered, "You can soon master it, if you stick to it, as I am doing. I do a bit each day."

THE PSALMES
OF DAVID TRANS
LATED ACCORDYNG

to the veritie and truth of th*
Ebrue, wyth annotacions moste
profitable.

MORS MORTIS MEDI-

CINA ET VICTORIA.

COLOS. III.

Teach and admonishe one another, in Psal-
mes, praises, and spiritual songs, singing
in your harts with thanks geuing vnto
the lord.

M. D. LVII.

1557 Psalms. Geneva version with no printer or place given. Only two copies
known extant: the Bodleian, Oxford and this the Peterborough Cathedral Library
copy on permanent loan to Cambridge University Library.

This Renaissance concern for sources can be seen in the search for ancient manuscripts. The largest and best collection was that of Cardinal Bessarion, whose 746 manuscripts included 482 in Greek.[1] His gift in 1468 to St. Mark's Library, Venice, aided the Aldine press and scholars at nearby Padua to prepare many critical editions.

At Padua, Greek studies began in 1463 with Demetrius Chalcon dyles, whose *Discourse* outlines the significance of Greek study: "Since Latin Grammar is joined to Greek ... how can one have a complete grasp of it unless he knows Greek letters?"[2] The impact of the studies at Padua, especially from 1503-09 under Marcus Musurus, is well known.[3]

The Renaissance of 1300-1600 means many things to scholars;[4] but three perspectives by modern scholars are especially worth noting.

Hans Baron has determined that around 1400 in the city of Florence a civic crisis prompted the Chancellor Coluccio Salutati to begin a new kind of historical analysis. In his essay *On Tyranny,* Salutati analyzed Cicero's motives for opposing Caesar. This attack on ancient motives led Leonardo Bruni, Salutati's successor, to analyze Athen's greatness in terms of its defense of liberty against the Persians. The classics were used to promote civic resistance against the Milanese Visconti in 1402.[5]

Eugenio Garin concludes that the work of humanists gave evidence of common values and a new historical awareness. The ancients were studied as living men—which meant that though scholars' study was solitary, it was nevertheless committed to civic experience. They recognized that grammar and rhetoric improved men's capacity to communi-

1. H.A. Omont, "Inventaire de manuscrits grecs et Latins donnes a Saint-Marc de Venice par le Cardinal Bessarion en 1468," *Revue des bibliotheques* 4 (1894):129–87.

2. Deno J. Geanakoplos, "The Discourse of Demetrius Chalcondyles on the Inauguration of Greek Studies at the University of Padua in 1463," *Studies In The Renaissance* 21 (1974):131.

3. See Deno J. Geanakoplos, *Greek Scholars In Venice* (Cambridge: Harvard University Press, 1962), pp. 111–66.

4. See Wallace K. Ferguson's admirable sketch in *The Renaissance In Historical Thought* (Boston: Houghton Miffin, 1948).

5. Hans Baron, *The Crisis of the Early Italian Renaissance,* 2 vols. (Princeton: Princeton University Press, 1955).

cate, but the humanists eschewed logic which gave nothing more than techniques of analysis.

According to Paul Oskar Kristeller, whose point of view we will follow here, Renaissance humanism was a method of study in which the text was the main concern. Scholars asked, What did the text in its own language say about the intent of its author? This was asked of legal, medical, and historical texts, as well as theological works.

> The histories are correct in regarding most Renaissance philosophers as slaves of the word.... For the Renaissance "philosopher" was a man who read his authorities in the original language and who permitted no deviations of doctrine that were not sanctioned by the original language of the author.[6]

In short, these humanists interpreted texts strictly within the parameters set by the historical setting and linguistic composition of the texts themselves. That was radical enough for Arabic treatises on chess or Roman legal theories; when applied to theology and the Holy Writ the results were explosive.

We must restrict our account of humanist commentators on Holy Writ to three: Giannozzo Manetti, whose Hebrew manuscripts founded the Vatican collection; Lorenzo Valla, whose work pioneered modern New Testament criticism; and the Dutch scholar Desiderius Erasmus, whose text became the first published Greek New Testament.

Giannozzo Manetti (1396-1459)

Manetti began his reading of the Old Testament for the first time on November 11, 1442. The Hebrew manuscripts in his possession included the Old Testament, Rabbi David Kimchi's commentaries, Abraham ibn Ezra, Salomon Isaaci, and Levi Gersonid. In 1454 Manetti composed his *Contra Iudeas et Gentes* in which he sought to point out the past errors of Jews. He also attempted to prove that one can know from the New Testament that Christ is the true Son of God.[7]

---

6. Neal W. Gilbert, *Renaissance Concepts of Method* (New York: Columbia University Press, 1960), p. 36.

7. See Charles Trinkhaus, *In Our Image and Likeness,* 2 vols., (Chicago: University of Chicago Press, 1970), 2:578–601. Trinkhaus depends on the pioneering study by S. Garofalo, "Gli umanisti italiani del secolo XV e la Bibbio," *Biblica* 27 (1946):338–75.

In 1455 King Alfonso of Naples took Manetti into his council and gave him a palace with a large staff of secretaries. In three years Manetti translated the New Testament and the Psalter. His preface to King Alfonso is worth citing:

> For since the true and solid foundations of both (ancient) and modern theology (as I would call it), by the agreement of all learned men, are contained only in the books of the Old and New Testaments, and I daily hear both of them, as translated from the true sources of the Hebrews and the Greeks into the Latin language by those from whom we have received them, criticised and torn to shreds, I have no longer been able to bear and tolerate this peaceably according to my strength. Especially influenced by this reason I have recently undertaken not improperly the labour of a new translation of both Testaments, although, whatever else it is, it is certainly a great and arduous task. . . . [8]

Manetti placed his "almost literal" version alongside Jerome's two versions. (It is a pity that Manetti's scholarship in these Vatican manuscripts has not been assessed by scholars who also know Hebrew.)

The translations of the New Testament and Old Testament Psalter are early witnesses to the humanist concern for Holy Writ. The wider impact of these pioneer studies came with the Erasmian Greek text of 1516 and Daniel Bomberg's second Hebrew Bible of 1524/25, printed in Venice.

After the fifteenth-century scholars like Ambrogio Traversari translated patristic literature from the early centuries of Greek and Latin Christianity. Fresh Latin versions of Scripture soon joined Jerome's Vulgate and a host of vernacular translations emerged in English, Italian, German, Catalan, French, and the languages of the Low Countries. Johann Mentel of Strasbourg published a German translation sometime before 1462, a version which had fourteen printings by 1507.[9] Italian biblical manuscripts appeared as early as the fourteenth century in Siena, Florence, and Venice. Two complete Bibles were printed at Venice in 1471; the first, compiled by Niccolo Malermi, became very popu-

---

8. Trinkaus, *In Our Image and Likeness,* 2:583.

9. Willem Jan Kooiman, *Luther and the Bible* (Philadelphia: Muhlenberg Press, 1961), p. 5.

lar.[10] So, we see that the Scriptures were known and published in
several languages prior to 1517.

Lorenzo Valla (1407-1457)

The Italian philologist Lorenzo Valla comes into our account because his *Notes on the New Testament* was discovered by Erasmus in
1504, and published in 1505. Several recent Italian biographies have
restored Valla to his role as the father of modern New Testament
criticism. The best of these biographies is by Salvatore Camporeale,
who devotes 126 pages to Valla's New Testament critique.[11] The
extensive information now available on Valla enables us to describe his
work with great precision.[12]

Humanists who compared the Greek and Hebrew texts with the
Latin and other extant versions revolutionized theological understanding. All too often, scholars today overlook the finer points of
grammatical analysis; for Valla that task was the most important a
Christian scholar could undertake. Erasmus himself defended Valla's
philological approach:

> For even if grammar is somewhat lower in dignity than other
> disciplines, there is no other more necessary. She busies herself
> with very small questions without which no one progresses to the
> large. She argues about trifles which lead to serious matters.[13]

Valla's philological interests separate him from the pre-Gutenberg
biblical commentators because his correction of the Vulgate represents
a new departure in biblical study. It may not be entirely accurate to
speak about Valla's Paulinism (as does Camporeale), but Valla did appeal to St. Paul in the famous *Adnotationes* (1453-1457), published by
Erasmus.

---

10. Kenelm Foster "Vernacular Scriptures in Italy," in *The Cambridge History of
the Bible,* 2:452–53.

11. Salvatore Camporeale, *Lorenzo Valla Umanesimo e Teologia* (Florence: Nella
Sede Dell' Istituto Palazzo Strazzi, 1972), pp. 277–403.

12. Jerry Bentley, "Lorenzo Valla: Biblical Philologist" (unpublished 1975 pa-
per).

13. Albert Rabil Jr., *Erasmus and the New Testament: The Mind of a Christian
Humanist* (San Antonio: Trinity University Press, 1972), p. 59.

Valla consulted at least seven Greek and four Latin manuscripts while noting variant readings. This led him to change the Vulgate text at I Corinthians 15:51 which read, "We all shall rise, but shall not be changed."[14] Valla corrected the Latin text from the Greek and showed that Paul's other statements support this, as in the very next verse (I Cor. 15:52) and in I Thessalonians 4:14-17.

Although at I Corinthians 15:51 the literary scholar only mended the superstructure of Scripture to better accommodate divine matters, he cited major cracks in the Vulgate version of Romans. Valla's primary intent can be seen in his work on Romans 1:17, for he neither commented on faith nor followed the usual medieval exegesis which interpreted the phrase "from faith to faith" to mean Old Testament faith leading to New Testament faith. Valla simply changed the Vulgate "is living" to a correct translation of the Greek future tense: "shall live."

Valla criticized exegetes such as Haimo of Auxerre, the ninth-century commentator used by Peter Lombard. Valla expands this criticism into an attack on Thomas Aquinas in the *Adnotationes* where he writes, "Why did not Paul advise him [Aquinas] of his errors, including among other things, his ignorance of the Greek language?"[15]

Valla corrected the Vulgate at Romans 8:28 which read, "We know that all things work for good to those who love God, those who are called and sanctified according to his purpose." Valla realized that this reading was debatable, since in the Greek text "all things" can be the subject of "works together" or its object. But St. Paul has already noted (in Rom. 7) that all things do not work for good for the Christian. So, on a theological/psychological basis, Valla decided to offer this grammatical ambiguity: God's Spirit works for good in all things whether good or evil for the 'called one.'[16]

Valla's *Elegantiae* on the Latin language was a rare piece of erudition for the late Renaissance, and his *Declamatio* on the *Donation of Con-*

---

14. Lorenzo Valla, *Adnotationes* (Paris: Johan Petit, MCV), sig. F iii r°: "Omnes quidem resurgemus sed non omnes immutabimur."

15. See my "Laurenzo Valla: Renaissance Critic and Biblical Theologian," *Concordia Theological Monthly* 39 (1968):23. Also Bentley, "Lorenzo Valla: Biblical Philologist," p.18–20.

16. See my "Lorenzo Valla: Renaissance Critic," pp. 25–26.

stantine (exposing it as a forgery) best combined his religious and rhe-
torical interests. In comparison with these works, the New Testament
Collatio and *Adnotationes* seem pedantic and unimportant (though to
be sure they sound a warning against the abstract concerns of systematic theology). But Valla's method was his message—and his influence
was enormous in the sixteenth century.

Valla was the first pure philologist of modern times to handle the
Greek text of the New Testament. It may be true, to borrow a phrase
from Roland Bainton, that "without warmth of committment scholarship is barren"; but it is also true that "without coolness of judgment
the results are unreliable."

Desiderius Erasmus (1469-1534)

The brilliant Dutch scholar Erasmus first visited England in 1499,
where he met John Colet of Cambridge, Dean of St. Paul's in London.
(Colet had given a dramatic series of lectures on Romans and I Corinthians at Oxford in 1496. He was among the first at Oxford to lecture
on Paul's epistles in the new fashion.)[17] In their discussion, Colet and
Erasmus argued about the interpretation of Christ's prayer in Gethsem-
ane. Erasmus thought Christ agonized over his imminent death, thereby
displaying His true humanity. Colet disagreed, based on Matthew
26:39, where Christ prayed that the cup might pass from Him if it were
the Father's will. Colet thought Christ wept not to save his own life,
but for Jerusalem and the nation. Erasmus' concern for personal cour-
age and Colet's defense of Jerome both indicate respect for the Scripture text and the attitudes of the Gospel writers rather than the doctrinal tradition.

As a result of this meeting, Colet invited Erasmus to lecture on
Moses or Isaiah while he was lecturing on Paul. Erasmus declined; in his
refusal he explained to Colet: "I am well aware how scant is my equip-
ment. . . . How can I have the effrontery to teach what I have not
learned? How shall I warm up others when I am myself shivering?"[18]

---

17. W. Robert Godfrey, "John Colet of Cambridge," *Archiv für Reformation-
sqeschichte* 65 (1974):6–17. Also P. Albert Duhamel, "The Oxford Lectures of
John Colet," *Journal of the History of Ideas* 14 (1953):493–510.

18. Rabil, *Erasmus and the New Testament,* p. 44.

In 1504 Erasmus wrote to Colet: "Three years ago I wrote something on St. Paul's Epistle to the Romans and finished with a single effort some four volumes, which I would have continued if I had not been hindered, my principle hindrance being my constant want of Greek."[19] Erasmus studied Greek for three years at Colet's inspiration and then discovered in 1504 the manuscript of Valla's *Notes on the New Testament.* Of course, Erasmus used his Greek for classical sayings and editions of the Greek church fathers, but his new concern was about literature more Christian than classical (this interest is evident in a letter Erasmus wrote to James Batt in December of 1500). For some time Erasmus longed to devote himself entirely to the study of sacred literature.[20]

This devotion of the Dutch humanist to Holy Writ had three important results. First was Erasmus' hastily produced Greek New Testament of 1516 with its fresh Latin translation, followed by editions of the church fathers whose exegesis became part and parcel of Reformation controversy.[21] Then came the notes and paraphrases of the New Testament text. Two items concern us here: the notes on Romans and the *Paraphrases.*

With the Greek text of 1516 and its notes, Erasmus paused to enrich the arid theology around him. For example, there is his well-known correction of the Vulgate at Matthew 3:2. To "do penance" was changed to read, "Come to a right mind, or return to reason."[22] Even more portentious was the Erasmian attack on the Latin theologians' misunderstanding of original sin (they mistranslated Romans 5:12). The Vulgate read "in whom all sinned," mistranslating the Greek "by which thing all sinned." Erasmus further observed that theologians were mistaken who claimed that "regeneration comes in the baptismal font."[23]

The notes on Romans expanded upon the paraphrase published in 1517. Erasmus intended a full Romans commentary as late as 1516, for

---

19. Ibid., p. 461.

20. Ibid., p. 48.

21. John C. Olin, "Erasmus and the Church Fathers," (Lecture given to the Sixteenth Century Studies Conference, University of Iowa, 1 November 1975).

22. Erasmus, *Annotationes* (Basel: Froben, 1540), p. 18.

23. Ibid., p. 366.

his note on Romans 1:11 in the 1516 New Testament promised an expansion. By 1527 the commentary included over seventy references to John Chrysostom.[24] In his analysis of Romans 6, Erasmus was careful to show that baptism marks only a beginning of progressive sanctity for Christians. Origen saw baptism as the start of a spiritual battle, and Erasmus concurred. He viewed the Christian as a soldier fortified by Christ the model of obedience and Abraham the singular example of faith.[25]

Erasmus even allowed some speculative allegorization, as when he approvingly noted Jerome's views on Matthew 3:12—where John the Baptist advised that a stronger and more worthy one was coming who would baptize in the spirit and fire. For Jerome this "fire" was to be understood in three ways: as the Holy Spirit in the guise of fiery tongues on the day of Pentecost; as the fire of persecutions and the cross; as the warmth of evangelical grace, contrasted with the cold Jewish ceremonies.

Without doubt, then, Erasmus set great store by spiritual interpretations of Scripture. We would be far off course, however, did we not note also the limits he placed on interpretations other than the literal. In fact, in the *Annotations* on the Gospels, Erasmus' attitude emerges on the whole as one of caution and restraint in employing para-literal analysis. It is not surprising, of course, that Erasmus should reject the more esoteric modes of analysis, such as numerical interpretation. But he disapproved also of most attempts at spiritual exegesis which were not firmly grounded on the literal text, and he insisted that spiritualizing exegesis be kept as simple as possible.

Erasmus discussed patristic speculation on Matthew 13:23—where Jesus explains the parable of the sower saying that, of the seed that fell on the good earth, some produced thirty-, some sixty-, and some hundred-fold yields. Jerome took this text to mean that virgins returned an hundred-fold yield on their faith, widows a sixty-fold, and

---

24. John B. Payne, "Erasmus: Interpreter of Romans," *Sixteenth Century Studies and Essays II,* ed. Carl S. Meyer (St. Louis: Foundation For Reformation Research, 1971), p 9.

25. Ibid., pp. 26–27.

married Christians a thirty-fold yield. Others, Erasmus noted, gave first place to martyrs, second to virgins, and third to widows, "leaving no place for honorable marriage." Augustine's hierarchy was martyrs, widows, married persons. Erasmus did not disapprove of "pious diligence and reverent curiosity in Divine Letters," but he thought it much simpler to suppose that Jesus in this text referred to the best, the average, and the worst Christians. This interpretation was a far cry from going "as far as possible beyond literal meaning."

Furthermore, Erasmus recognized the value of patristic witnesses for establishing the text of the Gospels. Take the case of the *pericope de adultera* (John 7:53–8:11). Jerome confessed that it was not to be found in all Greek manuscripts; Chrysostom and Theophylact failed to mention it in their otherwise complete commentaries on John's Gospel; Eusebius of Caesarea thought it apocryphal. Erasmus noted all these opinions; he mentioned also his own belief that the pericope might be aprocryphal, suggesting by the way that many apocryphal things could well be true. He suggested further that John might have included it in a late edition of his Gospel. He was finally persuaded to accept the pericope on the grounds that many Greek manuscripts contained the story (though not always at John 7:53–8:11), and that the "consensus of the Church approves it as worthy of the Gospel."

Evidence from the fathers was not always decisive for Erasmus (one might say that he worked also on the principle of the pious reading or of ecclesiastical consensus), but patristic evidence was important enough to him at least to be cited and discussed. And toward the end of his life, as he lost faith in the accuracy of Codex Vaticanus and other Greek manuscripts, his estimation of the value of the Greek fathers rose accordingly.[26]

Tudor translation of Erasmus' paraphrases marked royal endorsement of biblical humanism. Queen Katherine Parr translated these books and entrusted the Gospel of John to the Princess Mary. King

---

26. Jerry Bentley, "Erasmus' *Annotationes In Novum Testamentum* and The Textual Criticism of The Gospels," *Archiv für Reformationsgeschichte* 67 (1976): 33–53.

Edward VI ordered the Paraphrases set up in English parish churches
alongside the Great Bible.[27]

Erasmus often spun a simple text into a delightful tale, as in this
version of Luke's account of Mary and Martha:

> The two sisters were equal in their love of the Lord, but differed
> in temperament. Mary was ravished by the word of the Master.
> Martha was flitting about the house that nothing should be lack-
> ing to perfect hospitality. Martha, well knowing that her sister
> could never be detached from the feet of Jesus, did not chide her,
> but in a way remonstrated with Jesus for so charming her that she
> neglected to do what needed to be done. 'Master,' she said, 'Don't
> you care that my sister leaves me to do all of this alone? Tell her
> to help me. I know she won't leave you unless you tell her to, so
> entrancing are your words. But the dinner must be made ready
> and one pair of hands is not enough.' Then the Lord, who was
> delighted with the devotion of both women, did not chide the
> attachment of Mary, nor did he blame the complaint of Martha,
> though he leaned to Mary. 'Martha, Martha!' he said, 'Don't be so
> worried about getting the dinner and all worked up about many
> things. Mary has chosen the better part, to forget the things of
> the body and to be concerned for the things of the soul. I am
> grateful to you for preparing the dinner for me and my disciples,
> but to save souls is my meat and drink. The things of the body
> will pass away when that which is perfect is come. At the same
> time those who do as you have done will not lose their reward.
> They feed the hungry, clothe the naked, visit the sick and enter-
> tain strangers. Nevertheless those who attend to the one thing
> needful do more. But let no one complain of another, for each
> serves according to the gift received from God.'[28]

These *Paraphrases* became part of the social fabric of Reformation
England.[29]

In his *Enchiridion* of 1501 Erasmus not only spoke to England but
aimed to call all European Christianity back to its senses:

---

27. Roland Bainton, "The Paraphrases of Erasmus," *Archiv für Reformationsgeschichte* 57 (1966):67–76. See also William P. Haugaard, "Katherine Parr: The
Religious Convictions of a Renaissance Queen," *Renaissance Quarterly* 22
(1969):346–359.

28. Bainton, "Paraphrases of Erasmus," p. 70.

29. Colin W. Field, *The State of The Church In Glouchestershire 1563* (privately
published survey of 1563 parish records).

You love learning: that's fine—if you love it for the sake of
Christ. But if you love it only that you may have knowledge then
you rest where you should have made steps forward. . . . Thirst
for Christ that you may more clearly understand the Christ per-
meating the mysteries of Scripture. . . . [30]

The textual commentary that developed through Manetti, Valla, and
Erasmus is only one aspect of the humanist hermeneutic; another is
confession of faith.[31]

CONFESSION

Erasmus confessed his faith in several ways.[32] The *Enchiridion* of
1501, written for the militant husband of a gentle lady, sets forth what
has been labeled the "Philosophy of Christ." A lovely confession lies in
these lines:

He is charitable who rebukes the erring, who teaches the ignorant,
who lifts up the fallen, who consoles the downhearted, who supports the needy. . . . Just as Christ gave Himself completely for
us, so also should we give ourselves for our neighbor.[33]

In 1523 Erasmus composed a devout treatise on the Lord's Prayer
which Margaret More Roper (daughter of Sir Thomas More) translated
into English.[34] It speaks of Erasmus' concern for confession and prayer
as well as exegesis or commentary. His devotional use of Scripture can

30. Raymond Himelick, *The Enchiridion of Erasmus* (Bloomington, Ind.: Indiana
University Press, 1963), p. 96.

31. Carol Maddison, *Marcantonio Flaminio: Poet, Humanist and Reformer* (London: Routledge and Kegan Paul, 1965), p. 144.

32. An important study by Thomas N. Tentler isolates Erasmus from Protestant
theology on the issue of forgiveness and consolation alone. See Tentler's "Forgiveness and Consolation in the Religious Thought of Erasmus," *Studies in the Renaissance* 12 (1965):110–33.

33. John P. Dolan, *The Essential Erasmus* (New York: Mentor-Omega, 1964),
p. 68.

34. "A deuout treatise vpon the Pater noster made fyrst in latyn by the moost
famous doctour mayster Erasmus Roterdammus/and tourned into englishe by a
yong vertuous and well learned gentylwoman of XIX. yere of age," reprinted in
Richard L. De Molen, *Erasmus of Rotterdam: A Quincentennial Symposium*
(New York: Twayne Publishers, Inc. 1971), pp. 97–124.

be confirmed by a selection from this treatise; the second petition, "Thy Kingdom Come," reads as follows:

> Graunt father of all myght/that they/whome thy goodnesse ones hath delyuered from the tyranny of synne/and assygned to dwell in thy royalme/maye by the benifitte of the same benygne goodnesse contynue/and stedfastly abyde in theyr liberte and fredome: and that noe leauynge and fayling from the and thy sonne/retourne agayne in the tyrannous seruice of the deuyll: and so bothe by thy sonne shall raigne in the to our welthy/ and thou in vs to thy glorie: for thou art glorified in our blysse/ and our blysse is of thy goodnesse. Thy sonne Jesus taught vs we shulde dispice the realme of this worlde/ whiche standeth all by rychesse/and is holde vp by garrisons/of men/by hostes and armour/which also whatsoeuer it doth/dothe by fierse cruelnesse: and he with the holy goost/ouercame the wycked spirite that ruled as chefe and heed in the worlde: afore he by innocency and purenesse of lyuyng/had the victorie of synne/by mekenesse venquesshed cruelnesse/by suffraunce of many dispitefull rebukes/recouered euerlastying glory/by his owne deth restored life/and by his crosse had triumphe vpon the wycked spirites. Thus wonderfully has thou father warred and ouercame: after this manner thou both triumphest and reignest in thy sonne Jesus/.[35]

In 1524 Erasmus wrote a dialogue called *An Inquiry Concerning Faith* and a sermon titled *Concerning The Immense Mercy of God.* The speakers in the *Inquiry* dialogue, Aulus and Barbatus, discuss Christian doctrine. Aulus asks Barbatus a series of questions about Scripture, finally confronting him with the crucial question, "Why did He rise to live again?" Barbatus answers:

> First of all, to give us a certain hope of our resurrection. Secondly, that we might know that He in whom we have placed the safety of our resurrection is immortal and shall never die. Finally, that we being dead to sin by repentance, and buried together with Him by baptism, should by His grace be raised up again to newness of life.[36]

---

35. Ibid., p. 111.

36. Dolan, *The Essential Erasmus,* p. 215.

Erasmus' 1524 sermon on *The Immense Mercy of God* identifies divine mercy with justification. No clearer example can be found of Erasmus' concern for forgiveness:

> Peter had ceased to follow the Lord when he was denied three times, but he soon returned. When he remembered Jesus' words, he began to weep bitterly. He had been untrue to himself, but when he returned to his right mind, he returned to Jesus. For Isaias says, "Remember this, and be confounded, and return to your right mind you transgressors". Peter remembered and returned to his right mind. His stony heart, from which a teardrop could not be squeezed, was replaced with a heart of flesh. Tears then gushed forth, bitter because of the pain of his repentance, but wholesome because of his restored innocence.[37]

When the young Cambridge reformer Thomas Bilney first read Erasmus' new Latin version of the Epistles he turned to I Timothy 1:15, where Erasmus altered the Vulgate "This is a faithful saying. . . ."

> At last I heard speak of Jesus even then when the New Testament was first set forth by Erasmus: which when I understood to be eloquently done by him, being allured rather by the Latin than by the word of God . . . and at the first reading (as I well remember) I chanced upon this sentence of St. Paul (O most sweet and comfortable sentence to my soul) in I Tim. i: "It is a true saying and worthy of all men to be embraced that Christ Jesus came into the world to save sinners, of whom I am the chief and principal." This one sentence, through God's instruction and inward working, which I did not then perceive, did so exhilarate my heart, being before wounded with the guilt of my sins, and being almost in despair, that even immediately I seemed unto myself inwardly to feel a marvellous comfort and quietness, insomuch that my bruised bones leaped for joy.[38]

CONTROVERSY

Controversy surrounded the humanist attention to Holy Writ, and often overshadowed such confessions of personal faith as Thomas Bil-

---

37. Ibid., p. 251.

38. E. Gordon Rupp, *Studies in the Making of the English Protestant Tradition* (Cambridge: At the University Press, 1947), p. 23.

ney's. Nevertheless, men like Erasmus continued their commentary on the text and confession of its certainty.

Much criticism centered around Erasmus' Greek text. It had not been carefully prepared—Erasmus had rushed it into print. And, undaunted that his source manuscripts lacked the final verses of Revelation, Erasmus had supplied the missing six verses by translating them into Greek from the Vulgate.

Cardinal Ximines' Alcala circle in Spain actually printed the first Greek Testament, in 1514. (However, publication was delayed by the death of the Cardinal, and the Pope did not grant the license until 1520.) Ximines' concern for the original languages of Scripture was evident when his College of San Ildefonso opened in July of 1508 with three chairs for study of Latin, Greek, and Hebrew.[39] The Cardinal's search for manuscripts led him, in fact, to the notable Hebrew codice from Toledo c. 1280 A.D. and to certain New Testament Greek manuscripts from the Vatican Library.

Alfonso de Zamora (1474-1545) assisted Ximenes. Zamora, Alfonso's birthplace, was the center of fifteenth-century Jewish learning, and the place where Alfonso gained the rudiments of his eventually great linguistic competence in Hebrew, Aramaic, and possibly Arabic.

Diego Lopez de Zúñiga (Stunica) also helped Ximenes, by scrutinizing production of the New Testament. As section five of the *Complutensian Polyglot,* this lovely volume contained the New Testament in Greek alongside of the Vulgate, gave a summary of Greek grammar, and as a special aid presented its reader with the first short lexicon of New Testament Greek words.[40] So we see that Erasmus was not alone in his concern about printed sources of the Greek New Testament.

Martin Dorp (1485-1525), Professor of Philosophy at the University of Louvain, wrote Erasmus, advising him to desist from his work on the New Testament. Dorp worried about the Vulgate corrections. After all, if the Vulgate were wrong then the Catholic Church had been deceived for centuries. Dorp claimed that discrepencies between Latin manu-

39. Basil Hall, "The Trilingual College of San Ildefonso and the Making of the Complutensian Polyglot Bible," *Studies in Church History,* ed. G. J. Cuming (Leiden: E. J. Brill, 1969), pp. 121–22.

40. Hall, "The Trilingual College of San Ildefonso," p. 142.

scripts and Greek codices must have come from schismatic Greeks who altered the text. He posited that because the scriptural texts were so altered, no Greek authority could be trusted. Dorp claimed that no one should rely on the writings of those who fell away from the Roman Church. Erasmus asked Dorp why, then, he gave textual authority to the works of Aristotle, who wasn't even Christian.[41] Erasmus contended that theologians who carped at his interest in Greek and Hebrew needed to remember Augustine and Origen, great doctors of the patristic church.

> I ask you, my dear Dorp, what can you do with such theologians? What would you pray for, except possibly a good doctor to cure their brains? And yet this is the sort of people that shout the loudest in the assembly of the theologians; and they are the men who decide the fate of Christianity. They fear and dread as though it were dangerous and destructive the very skill which St. Jerome and even aged Origen acquired for themselves at such great pains so that they might truly be theologians. Even Augustine, when he was an elderly bishop, lamented in his *Confessions* that as a young man he had shrunk from the study of those letters which would have been so useful in explaining Sacred Scripture. If there be any danger, I shall not fear the risk which men so wise have invited.[42]

The hellenist Stunica likewise could not accept the idea of errors in the Vulgate. That is why he saw Erasmus' version as an open condemnation of the church. Could not the Dutch scholar be content with notes rather than a new Latin version? In response, Erasmus wrote the *Apology to Stunica,* in which he explained his attitudes and asserted his belief in moderation.[43]

In 1518 Jacob Latomus (1475-1544) advocated that Greek was unnecessary to understand the New Testament. Latomus said, "God has not bound together His wisdom and His law with certain letters or

41. John C. Olin, *Christian Humanism and the Reformation* (New York: Harper and Row, 1965), p. 85.

42. Ibid., p. 83.

43. Marcel Bataillon, *Erasme et l'Espagne* (Paris: Librairie E. Droz, 1937), pp. 98–109.

apexes of any individual language."[44] Latomus observed that the
Arians, heretics of the fourth century, for all their knowledge of Greek
did not read Scripture rightly. Of all his critics, Erasmus appreciated
Latomus as "very erudite and elegant."

Dorp, Stunica and Latomus each attacked the new Latin version and
the Greek New Testament. In Latomus' words, Scripture was like a wax
nose which Erasmus would twist to shape his fancy.

Jacques Lefèvre D'Étaples (1455-1536)

Use of the new texts by scholars brought another type of criticism
to the fore, such as that mounted by Jacques Lefèvre D'Étaples, French
biblical scholar and humanist. Jacques Lefèvre D'Étaples, also called
Faber Stapulensis, was the greatest French humanist contemporary of
Colet and Erasmus. As John Olin puts it:

> Like them he was profoundly influenced by the humanism of
> Italy; like them he came to focus on the study of scripture and
> the early Fathers; like them he saw reform as flowing from a
> return to the Gospel, from a rediscovery of the Word of God and
> the purer faith of the primitive Church.[45]

Faber taught at the University of Paris, visited Italy in 1491-92 to
imbibe Plato and Aristotle, and then edited texts of Aristotle. But Holy
Scripture so seized his attention that in 1509 Faber issued the five-fold
Psalter (later used by Luther) and in 1512 published an edition of
Paul's Epistles. From 1521 to 1525 Faber joined his episcopal patron at
Meaux, a diocese some twenty miles east of Paris. There he produced
two masterpieces—the 1522 *Commentaries on the Four Gospels* and the
1523 French translation of the New Testament. In 1525 came the
Epistres & evangiles pour les cinquante & deuz sepmaines de l'an, a
collection of pericopes and homilies for the laity, and in 1527 appeared

---

44. Cited in W. Schwarz, *Principles and Problems of Biblical Translation* (Cambridge: At the University Press, 1955), p. 165.

45. John C. Olin, *The Catholic Reformation* (Westminster, Md.: Christian Classics, 1969), p 107. See the discussion of *Christiformitas* in Guy Bedouelle, *Lefevre D'Etaples et l'Intelligence des Ecritures* (Geneva: Librairie Droz, 1976), especially chapter 9, "Christus Dominus est Totius Scripturae Spiritus," pp. 227–30.

the *Commentaries on the Catholic Epistles.*[46] The theme of Faber's
biblical contribution resounds in the 1521 preface to the *Four Gospels:*

> O you who are truly chosen by God and especially dear to me in
> Christ! Whoever loves Our Lord Jesus Christ and His Word in
> perfect purity, these alone are truly Christian, a name holy and
> venerable, about which Ignatius said to the Magnesians: Whoever
> is called by any other name than this is not of God. For the Word
> of Christ is the Word of God, the Gospel of peace, liberty, and
> joy, the Gospel of salvation, redemption, and life—the Gospel of
> peace, I say, after perpetual war, of liberty after a most harsh
> slavery, of joy after incessant grief, of salvation after the greatest
> ruin, of redemption after a most wretched captivity, and finally
> of life after endless death. And hence it is called the Gospel,
> which means the herald of good tidings and of the infinite bless-
> ings awaiting us in heaven. But whoever does not cherish Christ
> and His Word in this way, how are they Christian? Take counsel
> therefore, good Christians and pious readers, and beseech the
> Lord of the Word, who is the Lord Christ, that His Word does not
> fall without fruit, but that throughout the world it bears fruit
> unto life everlasting, and that He himself, who is Lord of the
> harvest, sends new and eager works to the new harvest.[47]

Our interest lies in the controversy surrounding Faber's biblical work.

Sorbonne suspicion aborted the early French scriptural experiment
at Meaux, in spite of the fact that the sister of Francis I endorsed
Faber's efforts.[48] The Sorbonne theologians first attached Faber's Vulgate revisions, then his biblical interpretations, and finally accused
Faber of Lutheranism.[49]

One such charge involved the three Marys Magdalene. Here, behind a
seemingly unimportant question, lay the issue of liturgical authority.
Faber contended that the liturgical veneration of Mary Magdalene was

---

46. Ibid., p. 111.

47. Ibid., pp. 116–117. See Eugene F. Rice, Jr., *The Prefatory Epistles of
Jacques Lefevre d'Etaples and Related Texts* (New York: Columbia University
Press, 1972).

48. See Anthony Levi, "Humanist Reform in Sixteenth-Century France," *Hey-
throp Journal* 6 (1965):447–64. Also Walter Bense, "Noel Beda and the Humanist
Reformation at Paris, 1504-1534," (Ph.D diss., Harvard, 1967).

49. Richard Cameron, "The Charges of Lutheranism Brought Against Jacques
Lefevre D'Etaples (1520-1529)," *Harvard Theological Review* 63 (1970):119–50.

actually based on a composite of three women in the Gospels. He pointed out that Mary the sister of Martha, Mary from whom seven demons were cast out, and Mary the public sinner were separate persons.[50] Faber's four treatises on the subject met a bitter response, especially from the English bishop of Rochester, who wrote against him. In defense, Faber appealed to the historical method, which proves that a new consciousness pervaded biblical exegesis. Noel Beda of Paris answered that Scripture must rest on a four-fold exegesis; he claimed that Faber's appeal to the literal sense—that the Evangelists were writing history—was an unsure human invention.[51] So the Sorbonne faculty denounced the preaching of three Marys as scandal. According to the faculty preamble, if anyone can on his own authority impugn the traditions of the holy fathers, nothing certain or free from doubt is left to the church.

> We therefore lay it down that the opinion of Pope Gregory that the Mary Magdalene who was the sister of Martha and she who was the sinner were but one person. Writings to the contrary are not to be tolerated; and no one shall presume to maintain in public debate or in sermons that there was more than one.[52]

William Tyndale and Sir Thomas More

The long-winded exchanges between William Tyndale and Sir Thomas More were central to Tudor polemics.[53]

William Tyndale (c. 1494-1536) was educated at Magdalen Hall, Oxford and Cambridge. He became Tutor to a gentleman's family, and often debated about Scripture with visitors, who were frequently clergymen. Tyndale eventually travelled to London seeking episcopal patronage to translate Holy Writ. Finding none, he left England—never to

50. Richard Cameron, "The Attack on the Biblical Work of Lefevre D'Etaples, 1514-1521," *Church History* 38 (1969): 13–24. See also Anselm Hufstader, "Lefevre d'Etaples and the Magdalen," *Studies In The Renaissance* 16 (1969): 31–60.

51. Cameron, "Attack on the Biblical Work of Lefevre D'Etaples," p. 21.

52. Ibid., p. 23.

53. Ranier Pineas, *Thomas More and Tudor Polemics* (Bloomington, Ind.: Indiana University Press, 1968), pp. 36–119.

return. After considerable trouble, evading the authorities and printing in secret, Tyndale finally was able to publish his translation (of Erasmus' Greek text) in 1526. His was the first printed English New Testament. His lucid and crisp translations of Scripture pioneered English Bible printing.[54]

Sir Thomas More's attack on Tyndale's English New Testament typifies several controversies raging between the Reformers and Rome. (For example, More objected to Tyndale's translation of *ecclesia* as "congregation" instead of "church.")

On March 7, 1528, the bishop of London (Tunstall) asked More to refute the heresy expressed in Tyndale's *Parable of the Wicked Mammon.* The *Parables,* along with *Obedience of the Christian Man,* set forth Tyndale's controversial position for the sole authority of Scripture; he also held that Scripture should be made accessible to the people in their mother tongue.

More responded to Tyndale in a tract of June 1529 called a *Dialogue concernynge heresyes.* His first polemic in English claimed that the Catholic Church of his day descended directly from the New Testament. He used the familiar argument that if a new version were to replace the Vulgate, that would mean the Church had been in error for 1500 years. Tyndale's 1531 *An answere unto Sir Thomas Mores dialogue* contends that the clergy kept Scripture from the people. In it, Tyndale revealed his love for the primitive church where priests preached and people prayed, and all were informed by Scripture:

Where now we hear but voices without significations, and buzzings, howlings, and cryings, as it were the hallooing of foxes, or baitings of bears; and wonder at disguisings and toys, whereof we know no meaning. By reason whereof we be fallen into such ignorance, that we know of the mercy and promises, which are in Christ, nothing at all. And of prayer we think, that no man can pray but at church; and that it is nothing else but to say Pater noster unto a post: wherewith yet, and with other observances of

---

54. Robert Williams, "Patterns of Reformation in the Theology of William Tyndale," in *Christian Spirituality Essays In Honour of Gordon Rupp,* ed. Peter Brooks (London: S.C.M. Press Ltd., 1975), pp. 121–39. See also Jens G. Moller, "The Beginnings of Puritan Covenant Theology," *Journal of Ecclesiastical History* 14 (1963):46–67.

> our own imagining, we believe we deserve to be sped of all that
> our blind hearts desire.[55]

From there the controversy intensified until the shivering, coughing scholar who read Hebrew by candlelight was strangled in Belgium.

Henry VIII had More executed for his refusal to see the king's view of Leviticus and for refusing to sign the act giving Henry supremacy over the English church. That was in the early years of the Anglican middle way between Luther and Rome.

But, whether burned in Belgium for translating Scripture, or attacked in Spain for altering the Vulgate, the humanists met controversy head on. Erasmus seemed aware of the conflict when he stated that not all the obscurities and difficulties in the Scriptures could darken the way of salvation. To eliminate some of the difficulties, Erasmus introduced his Greek-Latin version of the New Testament with a *Paraclesis* and gave a few pages to a *Ratio,* or method of study. To begin with, explained Erasmus, one must reverence the New Testament rather than be curious about it. And a fair knowledge of Greek, Latin, and Hebrew is the first step toward catching the spirit of what one reads in Scripture:

> As to the Schoolmen, I had rather be a pious divine with Jerome than invincible with Scotus. Was ever a heretic converted by their subtleties?. . . . The divine is 'invincible' enough who never yields to vice or gives way to evil passions, even though he may be beaten in argument. That doctor is abundantly 'great' who purely preaches Christ.[56]

Teresa of Avila in the sixteenth century summed up humanist concern for Holy Writ when she said: "If I had been a priest I should have made a thorough study of Hebrew and Greek so as to understand the thought of God as he has vouchsafed to express it in our human language."

And, many Reformers could say with the uncommon Knight at the Black Bear Inn: "You can soon master it, if you stick to it, as I am doing. I do a bit each day."

---

55. William Tyndale, *An Answer To Sir Thomas More's Dialogue* (Cambridge: At The University Press, 1850), p. 11.

56. Frederick Seebolm, *The Oxford Reformers: John Colet, Erasmus, and Thomas More* (London: Longmans, Green, and Cob, 1913), pp. 330–31.

2 Word and Spirit at Wittenberg

Luther's New Testament Prefaces

"The twilight in a Flemish prison, where a shivering, coughing scholar peers at Hebrew words in the falling dusk"[1] is part and parcel of our story. In his *Pathway into the Holy Scripture,*[2] Tyndale wonders with Luther how any man could be "so blind to ask why light should be shewed to them that walk in darkness . . . where to stumble is the danger of eternal damnation."[3]

Tyndale expanded Luther's preface to Romans and included it in his revised New Testament of 1534. Here Englishmen read Scripture with Lutheran accents:

A Prologue
Upon the Epistle of St. Paul
to the Romans

'Forasmuch as this epistle is the principal and most excellent part of the New Testament and most pure evangelion,' that is to say,

---

1. Gordon Rupp, *Six Makers of English Religion 1500-1700* (London: Hodder and Stoughton, 1957), p. 13.

2. *A Pathway into the Holy Scriptures* expands Tyndale's preface to the 1525 English New Testament, translated from Luther's own German preface.

3. Cited in Robert Williams, "Patterns of Reformation in the Theology of William Tyndale," in *Christian Spirituality Essays,* p. 126.

glad tidings, and that we call gospel, and also is a light and a way
unto the whole scripture; I think it meet 'that every christian man
not only know it, by rote and without the book, but also exercise
himself therein evermore continually, as with the daily bread of
the soul. No man verily can read it too oft, or study it too well;
for the more it is studied, the easier it is; the more it is chewed,
the pleasanter it is; and the more groundly it is searched, the
preciouser things are found in it.' . . . Faith is a lively thing,
mighty in working, valiant, and strong, every doing, ever fruitful;
so that is it impossible that he who is endued therewith should
not work always good works without ceasing.

Faith is then, a lively and a stedfast trust in the favour of God,
wherewith we commit ourselves altogether unto God; and that
trust is so surely grounded, and sticketh so fast in our hearts, that
a man would not once doubt of it, though he should die a thousand times therefor. And such trust, wrought by the Holy Ghost
through faith, maketh a man glad, lusty, cheerful, and true-
hearted unto God and unto all creatures. [4]

Prefaces to New Testament translations, in which readers were provided
with capsules of the gospel to ensure an orthodox understanding, were
known since Jerome and the Vulgate of the fourth century. Luther's
New Testament prefaces continue to have significance, since they repre-
sent one way he commented on Holy Writ. His 1522 *Preface to the
New Testament* defines the New Testament as "a book in which are
written the Gospel and the promises of God, together with the history
of these who believe and of those who do not believe them." [5] Luther
goes on to make a clear distinction between the works and words of
Jesus:

If I had to do without one or the other—either the works or
preaching of Christ—I would rather do without his works than his
preaching; for the works do not help me, but his words give life,

4. "A Prologue Upon The Epistle of St. Paul To the Romans," *Doctrinal Treatises and Introductions To Different Portions of The Holy Scriptures By William
Tyndale, Martyr, 1536* (Parker Society, Cambridge: The University Press, 1848),
pp. 484–93.

5. E. G. Rupp and Benjamin Drewery, *Martin Luther* (London: Edward Arnold,
1970), p. 93.

as he himself says. Now John writes very little about the works of Christ, but very much about his preaching, while the other Evangelists write much of his works and little of his preaching; therefore John's Gospel is the one, tender, true chief Gospel, far, far to be preferred to the other three and placed high above them. So, too, the Epistles of St. Paul and St. Peter far surpass the other three Gospels—Matthew, Mark, and Luke. In a word, St. John's Gospel and his first Epistle, St. Paul's Epistles, especially *Romans, Galatians* and *Ephesians,* and St. Peter's first Epistle are the books that show you Christ and teach you all that it is necessary and good for you to know, even though you were never to see or hear any other book or doctrine. Therefore St. James' Epistle is really an epistle of straw, compared to them; for it has nothing of the nature of the Gospel about it. . . . [6]

In his preface to Romans, Luther sums up both his Scripture principle and Paul's argument:

But do you follow the order of this Epistle? Worry first about Christ and the Gospel, that you may recognise your sin and his grace; then fight your sin, as the first eight chapters here have taught; then, when you have reached the eighth chapter, and are under the cross and suffering, that will teach you the right doctrine of predestination, in the ninth, tenth and eleventh chapters, and how comforting it is. For in the absence of suffering and the cross and the danger of death, one cannot deal with predestination without harm and without secret wrath against God. The old Adam must die before he can endure this subject and drink the strong wine of it. Therefore take heed not to drink wine while you are still a suckling. There is a limit, a time, an age for every doctrine. . . . [7]

John Warwick Montgomery claims that Luther taught verbal inerrancy of the scriptural text.[8] It is true that in a 1531 sermon on John 16:16-23 Luther said: "St. Augustine, in a letter to St. Jerome, has put down a fine axiom—that only Holy Scripture is to be considered iner-

---

6. Ibid., p. 94.

7. Ibid., pp. 96–97.

8. John Warwick Montgomery, "Lessons From Luther On The Inerrancy of Holy Writ," *Westminster Theological Journal* 36 (1974):277–304.

rant."[9] Against Zwingli at Marburg (1529) Luther held to the literal meaning of 'This Is My Body.'

> If he were to command me to eat dung, I would do so, assured that it were good for me. The servant doesn't brood over the wish of his lord. One must close his eyes.[10]

According to Jaroslav Pelikan, Luther's literal endorsement of inerrancy was tied in part to a medieval view of physics. Pelikan states that Luther applied to the text his views of spatial ubiquity, which were in fact nothing more than the fragments of an outmoded, quasi-scientific world view.[11]

When we study Luther's prefaces we must indeed ask, How did Luther relate the ancient text to his world view and his time?[12] Does Luther's conviction of the infallible authority of his reduced canon mean the inerrancy of all twenty-seven New Testament books? There is little evidence that Luther used inerrancy at all as his mode of understanding biblical authority. Gerhard Ebeling, a modern-day editor of Luther's 1513-14 translation of Psalms, argues that Luther sought to reveal man's position before God rather than give verbal descriptions of the Deity.[13] This complex distinction also relates to Luther's differentiation between the *words* and the *works* of Jesus (Luther preferred words to works, and so chose the power of words over actions). The literal sense combined with the idea of moral-as-christological marks a new kind of interpretation of Scripture.

Montgomery concentrates on the "James reference," in which Luther questions whether James belongs alongside John and Romans in the canon of Scripture. Though Luther did find canonical deficiencies when he compared James with Paul, Montgomery claims this in no sense contradicts Luther's belief in the entire infallibility of Holy

9. Ibid., p. 281.

10. Donald J. Ziegler, *Great Debates of the Reformation* (New York: Random House, 1969), p. 79.

11. Jaroslav Pelikan, *Luther The Expositor: Luther's Works Companion Volume* (St. Louis: Concordia Publishing House, 1959), pp. 139–41.

12. Gerhard Ebeling, "The New Hermeneutics and The Early Luther," *Theology Today* 21 (1964-65):34–46.

13. Ibid., p. 34.

Writ.[14] By this Montgomery means that the subjectivity of Luther's canon-within-the-canon is balanced by his affirmation of authority for those books he preferred.[15] However, if a part is superior to the whole, how can the whole be equal to the part in any sense?

Werner George Kümmel endorses Luther's prefaces to the New Testament simply because Luther did help his readers to interpret the text.[16] Luther said: "See to it, therefore, that you do not make a Moses out of Christ. . . ."[17] Though such "help" may prevent a reader from interpreting the text for himself, Luther's purpose was to reinterpret Scripture in a fresh ecclesiastical context. Luther's verbal concern is particularly apparent in the *Preface to Romans,* but Ebeling points out that the existential reality which Luther found in Scripture was even more important here. Kümmel, on the other hand, emphasizes the ecclesiastical dimension in these prefaces.

Another facet of Luther's prefaces is the eschatological. He patently preferred words of promise to the historical works of Jesus. Ebeling points to the judgement theme—which ought not, however, to exclude the verbal aspects of Luther's exegesis. The 1535 *Lectures on Galatians* returns to this subject in the comments on Galatians 5:5, "For through the Spirit, by faith, we wait for the hope of righteousness." This 1535 commentary by the mature Luther mirrors his pastoral and personal concerns in the context of Christian hope:

> The comfort is this, that in your deep anxieties—in which your consciousness of sin, sadness, and despair is so great and strong that it penetrates and occupies all the corners of your heart—you do not follow your consciousness. For if you did, you would say: "I feel the violent terrors of the Law and the tyranny of sin, not only waging war against me again but completely conquering me. I do not feel any comfort or righteousness. Therefore I am not righteous but a sinner. And if I am a sinner, then I am sentenced to eternal death." But battle against this feeling and say: "Even though I feel myself completely crushed and swallowed by sin

---

14. J. W. Montgomery, "Lessons From Luther," pp. 296–99.

15. Ibid., p. 300.

16. Werner George Kümmel, "The Continuing Significance of Luther's Prefaces to the New Testament," *Concordia Theological Monthly* 37 (1966):573.

17. Ibid., p. 574.

and see God as a hostile and wrathful judge, yet in fact this is not true; it is only my feeling that thinks so. The Word of God, which I ought to follow in these anxieties rather than my own consciousness, teaches much differently, namely, that 'God is near to the brokenhearted, and saves the crushed in spirit' (Ps. 34:18). And here Paul then teaches that through the spirit, by faith, those who are justified do not yet feel the hope of righteousness but still wait for it.[18]

Luther knew that in the midst of life's struggles, and during personal tragedy it is the Word of God which consoles and saves.

Let us learn, therefore, that amid great and horrible terrors, when the conscience feels nothing but sin and supposes that God is wrathful and Christ is hostile, we must not consult the consciousness of our own heart. No, then we must consult the Word of God, which says that God is not wrathful, but that He has regard for those who are afflicted, are contrite in spirit, and tremble at His Word (Isa. 66:2), and that Christ does not turn away from those who labor and are heavy-laden (Matt. 11:28) but revives them.[19]

The existential, ecclesiological, and eschatological dimensions in Luther's writings prove the richness of his mind and spirit. The gospel had seized Luther and he began, like Jack in the bean-stalk tale, to climb new heights and fight new giants. However, in that strange new land of the Bible Luther wrestled not against flesh and blood, but against principalities and powers. He was content to let the Word do its work.

Luther on Psalms (1513-15)

Paul said, "The letter kills: the Spirit gives life." During twelve centuries of its history, the church had added several spiritual senses to the literal meaning of the biblical text. In the Psalms lectures of 1513-15 Luther departed from this medieval way of understanding Scripture.

German scholars have long observed that Luther clarified his hermeneutic by identifying the literal sense of Scripture with the tropological, or moral (which Luther understood as Christological). The mystical and

---

18. *Luther's Works,* ed. Hilton C. Oswald, vol. 27, *Lectures On Galatians, 1535* (Saint Louis: Concordia Publishing House, 1964), p. 26.

19. Ibid., p. 27.

futuristic senses were replaced by "justification by faith alone." Ebeling's classic 1951 essay argues that the groundwork lay in the 1513-16 period, and the actual break from medieval theology took place after 1516.[20] More recently, James Preus has argued that this Christological and tropological interpretation hindered Luther's discovery of justification by faith.[21] He claims that it was not until the 118th Psalm that Luther understood the meaning of promise as a future-oriented faith. Preus is not convincing. Stephen Ozment of Yale argues that Luther in the Psalms lectures was "struck by the way union with God was accompanied by the awareness of distance from God."[22] The bulk of the commentary on Psalm 50 is carried away by this correlation. Conditioned salvation was executed by faith and hope, not by love as in scholastic theology. So Ozment sees Luther's view of existence having specific *termini* in its soteriological basis. It remembers past works of God and hopes in future works of God. To forget the manifest past works of God is, for Luther, to forfeit confidence in promised future works. These past and future works of God form a haven where the whole man can take refuge. Luther was confident that though death and sin destroy all temporal ground on which to stand, God chooses to support a sinner by memory and hope.[23]

Luther's notion of faith in the Psalms lectures of 1513-15 already correlates faith with the promises of God. Luther considers these promises certain simply because they are made by God. Luther here is not only future-oriented but he is unconcerned with human wisdom. Even the synagogue in Old Testament times longed for the saving act of God on the cross as promise and fulfillment. David's Psalms express that hope for Luther.

---

20. Gerhard Ebeling, "Die Anfange von Luthers Hermenutik," *Zeitschrift für Theologie und Kirche* 48 (1951): 172–230 revised in *Lutherstudien* I (Tübingen, 1971), pp. 1–68. See especially pp. 6–7.

21. James S. Preus, *From Shadow to Promise: Old Testament Interpretation From Augustine to the Young Luther* (Cambridge: Harvard University Press 1969). See alternate view in Scott Hendrix, *Ecclesia in Via* (Leiden: E. J. Brill, 1974), pp. 263–287.

22. Stephen Ozment, "Luther and the Late Middle Ages: The Formation of Reformation Thought," in *Transition and Revolution,* ed. Robert M. Kingdon (Minneapolis: Burgess Publishing Company, 1974), p. 126.

23. Steven Ozment, *Homo Spiritualis* (Leiden: E. J. Brill, 1969), pp. 109–111.

The Preface of Jesus Christ sets forth Luther's intent to read the ancient Hebrew Psalter as a series of promises fulfilled in Christ. Luther in this preface to his Psalms lectures claims four witnesses to God's presence among His people. The first witness is Moses from Exodus 33:14, 15. Zechariah 9:1 next testifies that the Lord is the eye of man and of all the tribes of Israel. Peter testifies in Acts 3:24 that all prophets from Samuel proclaimed these days [of the Spirit]. Finally, Luther points to the apostle Paul who in I Corinthians 2:2 decided to know nothing except Jesus Christ crucified. In this preface Luther added the famous gloss:

> *Psalm 34:5:* 'Look to Him, and be radiant; and your faces will never be ashamed.' But others make a detour and purposely, as it were, avoid Christ, so do they put off approaching Him with the text. As for me, when I have a text that is like a nut with a hard shell, I immediately dash it against the Rock and find the sweetest kernal.[24]

Luther's first guideline is that

> every prophecy and every prophet must be understood as refering to Christ the Lord, except where it is clear from plain words that someone else is spoken of. For thus He Himself says: 'Search the Scriptures, . . . and it is they that bear witness to me.'[25]

Luther's Romans (1515-16)

A copy of Luther's 1516 lectures first appeared in print in 1899. The Vatican librarian used it to show that Luther's exegesis of Romans 1:17 was no different from the medieval church's understanding of faith. (Protestant scholars were a bit nervous about this Vatican manuscript.) Then, incredibly enough, Luther's original copy of the Romans lectures appeared in a showcase in the Royal Library in Berlin. The critical Weimar edition of these lectures began the modern renaissance of Luther research.[26] The lectures had not been available to students of the Reformation for 350 years.

---

24. *Luther's Works,* ed. Hilton C. Oswald, vol. 10, *First Lectures on the Psalms: Psalms 1-75* (St. Louis: Concordia Publishing House, 1974), p. 6 n. 3.

25. Ibid., p. 7.

26. Gordon Rupp, *The Righteousness of God* (London: Hodder and Staughton, 1953), pp. 158–59.

Luther's *Romans* marks a Copernican revolution in his understanding of God. Gordon Rupp reminds us:

What we have is no mere written commentary, but that they were expounded with ardent (and sometimes drowsy) eloquence in the early morning, as the days and months rolled on, from the dim chilly hours of winter to the warm drenching sunshine of the summer, to an audience which, like all academic audiences in all times and in all places, rendered attention fitfully, always eager to be distracted by a gust of wind or a vagrant butterfly.[27]

Until Luther, medieval Bible commentators had used a four-fold system of analysis. They found in many passages a literal sense, which taught what happened; an allegorical sense, which taught what must be believed; a moral sense, which taught what must be done; and an anagogical sense, which taught what must be hoped.

But one can read in Luther's impressive lectures on Romans a fresh understanding of the grace, mercy, and justice of God. In a sermon on St. Thomas Day, 21 December 1516, Luther preached about the alien work of God as Isaiah 28:21 says: "The strange work of the gospel is to prepare a people perfect for the Lord, that is, to make manifest sins and pronounce guilty those who were righteous in their own eyes."[28] Luther concluded that the proper work of the gospel produces Christians by showing them how misfortunate they are.

The 1515-16 Romans rebukes those theologians who teach that if a man does the best he can, God is bound to reward him with grace. Luther insisted that man cannot fulfill the intent of the law. Nominalism taught that absolutely God freely forgives, but ordinarily speaking He cooperates with a man's best efforts to please God. Luther recalled that while he was in the monastery he could not understand that though he had made his confession he was still a sinner:

I thought that all my sins were taken away and removed, even the inward sin . . . thus I fought with myself, not knowing that the remission was indeed a fact, but that there was no taking away save in hope. . . . That is why those are mere ravings which say that a man by his own powers can love God above all things, and

27. Ibid., p. 159.

28. *Luther's Works,* vol. 51, (American ed.), pp. 17–23.

do the works prescribed, 'according to the substance of the deed, but not according to the intention of the lawgiver, because not done in grace'. O Fools, O Sowtheologians![29]

In these lectures one sees Luther departing from medieval use of Scripture to a fresh understanding of faith. It was not his knowledge of the Greek language or the application of the literal sense which led Luther to add *sola* to the text of Romans 3, but a fresh sense of God's grace and mercy. *Sola fide* (by faith alone) became a slogan of early Protestant exegesis.

The theology of the cross based on the two-fold distinction between the alien work of God in Isaiah 28:21 and the proper work of Christ in I Corinthians 1 pervades Luther's writings. *The Heidelberg Disputation* of 1518 and the *Explanation of the Ninety-Five Theses* develop this theme theologically.

Luther's Hebrews (1517-18)

Let us turn briefly to the fine *Commentary on Hebrews* of March 1517–March 1518. (We are dependent on student copies which are, fortunately, reasonably complete.) I agree with Gordon Rupp that they contain some of Luther's finest utterances. They rely on St. Chrysostom and reflect a growing mastery of Greek, based on the texts of Erasmus.

During the quiet first term of that year, Luther lectured two days a week (Monday and Friday) from 6 to 7 a.m. The next term, however, saw the posting of the ninety-five theses which made the Wittenberg lecturer famous overnight and threatened on every side.

As Luther simultaneously approached chapter eleven of Hebrews and the Heidelberg meeting of his Augustinian order, faith became the key concept. Excitement mounted through the weeks, and so did the pressure on Luther. He wrote, "We are a house, which Christ builds, but this act of building is nothing else than the tension and pressure and all the cross and sufferings which are in Christ."[30] The works of the law are external, said Luther, while the work of the gospel is internal faith.

---

29. Rupp, *Righteousness of God,* pp. 176–77.

30. Ibid., p. 204.

For thus by the Spirit we are freed from the law, not that it should not exist, but that it should not be feared, and thus we are freed from the Devil, not that he should not be, but that we should not be afraid of him, and so from death, not that death should not be, but that he should be feared.[31]

Kenneth Hagen finds in Luther's *Hebrews* four basic elements of faith. Faith comes from hearing the Word; it cleanses the heart; it possesses things hoped for; and it is the certitude of salvation.[32] Luther's struggle for faith caused him to oppose the medieval exegetes who misread in Hebrews 11:1-2 such rational terms as *substance* and *evidence*. Luther claimed that reason could never do what faith did for the heroes of Hebrews 11. Faith is possession of the Word.[33] Luther's powerful exegesis led him to several magnificent conclusions in these lectures:

We Christians ought to learn how to die with joy for it is impossible that Christ, the victor of death, should die again, so it is impossible that he that believeth in him should die. . . . Whoever fears death or does not want to die is not yet a sufficient Christian, for he fails in resurrection faith, so long as he loves this life more than that which is to come. . . .[34]

Who would not be moved by these noble words from a set of sixteenth-century student notes? No breeze or butterfly could distract a student whose teacher could say:

O it is a great thing to be a Christian man and have a hidden life, hidden not in some cell, like the hermits, or even in the human heart, which is an unsearchable abyss, but in the invisible God himself, and thus to live in the things of the world, but to feed on him who never appears except in the only vehicle of the hearing of the Word.[35]

---

31. Ibid., pp. 205–206.

32. Kenneth Hagen, *A Theology of Testament in the Young Luther: The Lectures on Hebrews* (Leiden: E. J. Brill, 1974), p. 82.

33. Ibid., p. 86.

34. Rupp, *Righteousness of God,* p. 207.

35. Ibid., p. 33.

Indeed, it was the preface to the Romans lectures which warmed John Wesley's heart at Aldersgate and the mature Galatian commentary which converted Charles Wesley. Luther's concept of Christ, faith, and hearing of the Word mark these commentaries as remarkable sixteenth-century expositions of Scripture.

Luther's influence spread from the sixteenth century to the seventeenth, and from Saxony to an Anglo-Saxon in Bedford. John Bunyan, sick of soul in his own search for grace, describes his despair in *Grace Abounding:*

> Well, after many such longings in my mind, the God in whose hands are all our days and ways, did cast into my hand, one day, a book of Martin Luther, his comment on the Galathians, so old that it was ready to fall piece from piece if I did but turn it over. Now I was pleased much that such an old book had fallen into my hand; the which, when I had but a little way perused, I found my condition in his experience, so largely and profoundly handled, as if his Book had been written out of my heart: this made me marvel: for thus thought I, this man could not know anything of the state of Christians now, but must needs write and speak of the Experience of former days. Besides, he doth most gravely also, in that book debate of the rise of these temptations, namely, Blasphemy, Desperation, and the like. . . . I do prefer this book of Mr. Luther upon the Galathians, (excepting the Holy Bible) before all the books that ever I have seen, as most fit for a wounded Conscience.[36]

CONFESSION

A survey of Luther's letters, catechisms, hymns, and other confessional documents reveals his amazing wisdom. And such a survey would be one way to trace the impact of the Bible in the sixteenth century. In order to understand biblical study at Wittenberg, we must turn to Philip Melanchthon, who wrote the 1530 *Augsburg Confession* and was Luther's Greek professor and confidant. In those early years there were

36. John Bunyan, *Grace Abounding to the Chief of Sinners,* ed. Roger Sharrock (Oxford: At The Clarendon Press, 1962), pp. 40–41.

no Lutherans, only Martinians; "Protestants before Protestantism—the time of the pioneers, when as yet the map-makers and the road makers had not appeared."[37]

Loci Communes (1521)

The audience wondered what the young Greek lecturer would say in his 1519 defense of the twenty-four theses at Wittenberg. Melanchthon, nephew of the famous Hebraist Reuchlin, had already given a stirring defense of the liberal arts at Tübingen in 1517. Luther endorsed the 21-year-old scholar who slipped him notes to counter Eck at the Leipzig Debate. Eck called Philip "The dusty schoolmaster."[38] Now, a year after coming to Wittenberg, the very popular teacher defended the liberal arts: "Dare to know, cultivate the ancient Latins, embrace Greek, without which Latin cannot be rightly pursued."[39]

As many as two thousand students crowded into Melanchthon's lectures. Luther urged Philip to lecture on Romans, stole his lecture notes and published them. This resulted in a 1519 *Theological Instruction* which adapted a new method of biblical exposition. Melanchton wrote a preface to Luther's Galatian commentary in which he mused on the rescue the book would bring to those shipwrecked on the sea of scholastic distinctions.[40] The method is crucial, and it appears in the first systematic statement of the Reformation—Melanchthon's *Loci Communes (Common Places)* of 1521. Published student notes on his Romans lectures of 1519 forced Melanchthon to state his views in more organized fashion. However, the complexities of the second *Loci* edition of 1535 and the final expansion in 1543-44 lie beyond our scope. At the end of his life, Luther said of this work:

---

37. Gordon Rupp, *Patterns of Reformation,* (London: Epworth Press, 1969) p. xiii.

38. Clyde Manschreck, *Melanchthon The Quiet Reformer* (Nashville: Abingdon Press, 1958), p. 49.

39. "On Improving the Studies of Youth," trans. Lewis Spitz, Sr., in *Transition and Revolution,* ed. Robert N. Kingdon (Minneapolis: Burgess Publishing Company, 1974), p. 170.

40. Robert Stupperich, *Melanchthon* (Philadelphia: Westminster Press, 1965).

> You cannot find anywhere a book which treats the whole of theology so adequately as the *Loci Communes* do. . . . Next to Holy Scripture, there is no better book.[41]

The three topics of this popular work are: sin, law, and grace. Under these topics Melanchthon set his material "to assist in one way or another, the studies of those who wish to be conversant with the Scriptures."[42] Melanchthon explained his method in the *Questions and Answers on Dialectic* (1547). He said that his purpose was not that of Aristotle who selected logical topics to investigate, but was instead similar to Cicero's dialectical/rhetorical purpose. In such a locus, one selects material because he already finds it convincing. Orderly selection confirms the truth rather than searches further for it.[43] Such a purpose was well-suited to Protestantism, which adopted the pulpit as its chief vehicle. A preacher could convince from the pulpit more readily if he in private had not doubts about the content of his message.

Melanchthon opens his topical theology with the famous lines:

> For from these things [the power of sin, the law, and Grace] Christ is known, since to know Christ means to know his benefits and not as they teach, to reflect upon his natures and the modes of his incarnation.[44]

These lines describe the three sections of his *Common Places.* Section one describes sin as "a state of mind contrary to God."[45] Melanchthon claimed that those theologians err who see sin as outward acts; sin is not a weakness to be overcome by human power but is a fatal disease which only the Spirit of God can heal.

In section two of the *Common Places,* Melanchthon describes law as giving sin power over persons. Law commands the good and forbids the bad. Therefore, the evangelical commands in Matthew 5 to love one's

---

41. Wilhelm Pauck, *Melanchthon and Bucer* (Philidelphia: Westminster Press, 1969), p. 17.

42. Manschreck, *Melanchthon The Quiet Reformer,* p. 84.

43. Quirinius Breen, The terms 'Loci Communes' and 'Loci' in Melanchthon," *Church History* 16 (1947):204–205.

44. Pauck, *Melanchthon and Bucer,* pp. 21–22.

45. Ibid., p. 47.

enemies, forgive one another, and so forth, are demands of the law. Melanchthon pointed out that men who think these lists enable them to keep the law are, in fact, sick men. Their false view turns commands into suggestions, and deceives them.[46]

Grace, or the Gospel, in Melanchthon's third section is "the promise of the grace or mercy of God, especially the forgiveness of sins and the testimony of God's goodwill toward us."[47] This theology of promise extends Luther's theology of the cross in the direction of consolation in Christ's benefits.

Hence the Bible at Wittenberg was understood as a Word of condemnation and consolation, a theology of the cross contrasted with a theology of glory. Luther and Melanchthon exposed the gospel which centuries of study had obscured beyond all recognition.

Patristic Argument

Scholars have long known that Scripture alone was not the main issue separating Rome from the Reformers. Central to the schism was the patristic argument—which Erasmus furthered by his magnificent editions of the church fathers. Exploring the use of patristic literature in the sixteenth century leads us directly to the Reformers. Appeal to Scripture, and the new understanding of faith, meant at a deeper level the proper understanding of patristic literature. The Reformers in this way tried to pass over medieval theology and return to the early church fathers, as corrected by the new scriptural principle.

The use of handbooks for quotations suitable in theological discussion is based on ancient tradition. Biblical scholars know of such effort on the part of New Testament redactors.[48] That Paul used such testimonia has led modern exegetes to a fuller comprehension of Paul's theological program.

In the same way, Pierre Frankel's magnificent *Testimonia Patrum* (1961) explores the function of ancient opinion in sixteenth-century

46. Ibid., pp. 57–58.

47. Ibid., p. 71.

48. E. Earl Ellis, *Paul's Use of The Old Testament* (Edinburgh: Oliver and Boyd, 1957).

theology. In 1525 Melanchthon wrote Thomas Blauer that he had a collection of *Sententiae Veterum* supporting 'est' in the dispute over 'hoc est corpus meum.'[49] In 1529 a second collection appears in a chapter on Christology which found its way into the 1535 second edition of *The Common Places.*[50] The *Sententiae Veterum de Sacra Coena* (1530)[51] was mentioned in an open letter to the Swiss Reformer Oecolampadius in April of 1529.[52] Robert Barnes, Cambridge English Lutheran, prepared first among his writings a list of patristic quotations under nineteen headings. Barnes used the pseudonym Antonius Anglus for this 1530 work. (The Wittenberg imprint by J. Clug is titled Sen-/tenciae Ex Doc-/toribus Col-/lectae Qvas papistae ualde im-/pudenter hod-/die dam-/nant.) Barnes' 1531 *Supplication* expands the sentences on faith, free will, church, keys, councils, utraquism, human constitutions, saints, and images. The Lutheran Bugenhagen translated them into German (printed twice in 1531 and again in 1536) and they were reprinted in Latin in Barne's *Lives of The Popes* (1555, 1567) and as amended in 1558.[53]

More intriguing is the patristic handbook known as the *Unio dissidentium*, published under the pseudonym H. Bodius at Cologne in September of 1531. Robert Peters has traced its authorship to Strasbourg and the circle around Martin Bucer. Perhaps Kaspar Hedio, who made a German translation in 1537, was a chief compiler.[54] The first part was published in March 1527 by the Antwerp printer Martin de Keyser. Among ten sections of the first part are patristic passages on original sin, infant baptism, predestination, nature and function of law,

49. Pierre Fraenkel, *Testimonium Patrum: The Function of the Patristic argument in the Theology of Philip Melanchthon* (Geneva: E. Droz, 1961), p. 22.

50. Ibid., p. 23.

51. *Corpus Reformatorum* 23, ed. H. E. Bindsell (Brusvigoe: C. A. Schwetschke et Filium, 1855).

52. Pierre Fraenkel, "Ten Questions," in *Luther and Melanchthon in the History and Theology of the Reformation,* ed. Vilmos Vajta (Philadelphia: Muhlenberg Press, 1961), p. 157. [*C.R.* 1/1049].

53. William Clebsch, *England's Earliest Protestants: 1520-1535* (New Haven, Conn.: Yale University Press, 1964), pp. 49–50.

54. Robert Peters, "Who compiled the Sixteenth-Century Patristic Handbook *Unio Dissidentium?*" *Studies In Church History* 2 (1965):249–50.

Worms, troops of the Elector Frederick carried him off to the Wartburg. Luther's second castle experience was at the Coburg Castle, where he fretted while Melanchthon drafted the *Augsburg Confession.*

Protestantism originated in the protest submitted at the second Diet of Spires in 1529. Six princes and fourteen cities joined in an evangelical protest there on April 19. Things were far from hopeful as 1530 began, for the German electors were not even invited to watch the crowning of Charles V as Holy Roman Emperor at Bologna on February 24. Only the Turkish threat of Suleiman II's armies at the gates of Vienna prodded Charles to call a Diet at Augsburg for 8 April 1530.

Four hundred and four articles under Eck's preparation set the stage for Melanchthon's careful response at Augsburg. At seven a.m., June 16, the Protestant princes gathered before the Emperor with Margrave George of Brandenburg as chief spokesman. Between June 17 and 24 Melanchthon met with the Imperial secretaries to rework the Confession. At three in the afternoon of June 24, the German text was read aloud, with every Protestant delegate on his feet!

Luther chaffed in the Coburg Castle during these events. In several letters he urged Philip not to worry but trust the gospel. "God has set the matter," wrote Luther, "in a place which you can neither reach by your rhetoric nor by your philosophy. That place is called Faith. . . ."[58]

In twenty-eight articles, the *Augsburg Confession* illumines questions of faith based on justification. The *Apology,* prepared in August 1530 by Melanchthon, sharpens the focus of these questions. The *Augustana* and the *Apology* are twin confessions of biblical understanding in the early Reformation decades.

The *Augsburg Confession* defines "faith alone" in article XX as taught in Ephesians 2:8-9 and in Augustine. "His whole book, *De spiritu et litera,* proves this"[59] wrote Melanchthon. This double proof from Paul and the patristic arsenal was significant, especially since Melanchthon accused Rome of novelty.[60]

---

58. Manschreck, *Melanchthon The Quiet Reformer,* p. 195.

59. *The Book of Concord,* trans. and ed. Theodore G. Tappert (Philadelphia: Muhlenberg Press, 1959), pp. 42–43.

60. See the magnificent study by Pierre Fraenkel, *Testimonium Patrum.*

The *Apology* in Article IV defines justification:

> Paul clearly shows that faith does not simply mean historical
> knowledge but is a firm acceptance of the promise. . . . So it is
> not enough to believe that Christ was born, suffered, and was
> raised unless we add this article, the purpose of the history, 'the
> forgiveness of sins'. . . . these three elements always belong to-
> gether: the promise itself, the fact that the promise is free, and
> the merits of Christ as the price and propitiation.[61]

To know this promised mercy of God, claimed Melanchthon, is what it
means to know the benefits of Christ. Hence we see that in the discus-
sions of Word and Spirit at Wittenberg, not only Luther and Augustine
were interpreters of Paul, but so also was the brilliant Melanchthon.

Luther's Counsel and Catechism

To complete our study of the confessional aspect of Word and Spirit
at Wittenberg, we must glance at some of Luther's letters and the
shorter catechism. The tenderness of the pastor shines through the
letters.

John Staupitz was Luther's superior in the Augustinian Order;
Luther succeeded Staupitz as biblical lecturer in the new University of
Wittenberg.[62] A letter to Staupitz of 30 May 1518 thanks him for a
true understanding of penitence, which must begin with the love of
justice and God rather than end there as a method of confession. "Your
words on this subject pierced me like the sharp arrows of the
night. . . ."[63]

A letter to the court chaplain Spalatin of 15 August 1521 uses a
hunting trip as an allegory of salvation. Luther's party caught two
hares, one of whom Luther rolled up in the sleeve of his cloak. The
dogs found the rabbit, bit through the cloak and killed it. Luther wrote
to Spalatin:

---

61. *Book of Concord,* p. 114.

62. See David Steinmetz, *Misericordia Dei: The Theology of Johannes Von
Staupitz in its Late Medieval Setting* (Leiden: E. J. Brill, 1968).

63. Rupp and Drewery, *Martin Luther,* p. 10.

Hares and innocent creatures are captured by men, not by bears, wolves and suchlike Bishops and theologians; to be swallowed up by the latter means hell, but by the former heaven! . . . you courtiers, so keen on the chase, will yourselves be wild beasts in paradise, and even Christ, the supreme hunter, will have his hands full to catch and save you! While you are playing around hunting, you are being made game of yourselves. . . .[64]

The famous communique to Luther's wife Kattrina von Bora is a classic of confession:

To the saintly, anxious lady, Katherine Luther, owner of Zulsdorf, at Wittenberg, my gracious dear wife. Grace and peace in Christ! Most saintly lady doctoress, we thank you kindly for your great care for us, which prevented you sleeping, for since you began to be so anxious we were nearly consumed by a fire in our inn just outside my room door; and yesterday, doubtless on account of your anxiety, a stone fell upon our heads and almost crushed us as in a mouse-trap; and over and above, in our own private room, lime and mortar came down for two days, and when the masons came—after only touching the stone with two fingers—it fell, and was as large as a large pillow, and two handbreadths wide. We had to thank your anxious care for all this, but happily the dear, holy angels guarded us also. I fear if you do not cease being anxious the earth may at last swallow us up and the elements pursue us. Is it thus thou hast learnt the Catechism and the faith? Pray and leave it to God to care for us, as he has promised in the fifty-fifth Psalm and many other places, 'Cast thy burden on the Lord, and he shall sustain thee.'[65]

Next, we turn to catechism. The *Smaller Catechism* of 1529 has all of Luther in it. If all his works vanished save this one and the reply to Erasmus, said Luther, he would be content. Katherine is reported to have said, "It tells me all about myself." Luther wrote it for small children and said:[66] "I have to do just as a child and say word for word . . . the Lord's Prayer and the Ten Commandments, the Creed and the Psalms." In the end Luther taught a simple confession which a child

---

64. Ibid., p. 74.

65. Ibid., p. 171.

66. Roland Bainton, *Here I Stand* (New York: New American Library, 1956), p. 264.

could comprehend. On the first article of the Creed the *Smaller Cate-chism* asks:

> I believe in God the Father Almighty, Maker of heaven and earth. What does that mean?
> Answer: I believe that God has created me and all other creatures, and has given me, and preserves for me, body and soul, eyes, ears, and all my limbs, my reason and all my senses; and that daily he bestows on me clothes and shoes, meat and drink, house and home, wife and child, fields and cattle, and all my goods, and supplies in abundance all needs and necessities of my body and life, and protects me from all perils, and guards and defends me from all evil. And this he does out of pure fatherly and divine goodness and mercy, without any merit or worthiness in me; for all which I am bound to thank him and praise him, and, more-over, to serve and obey him. This is a faithful saying.[67]

Someone once questioned why philosophers find it more difficult to think than most men, and why theologians find it more difficult to believe. At Wittenberg Luther and Melanchthon taught theologians and pastors to share a lively faith.

CONTROVERSY

Rome

Luther fought a two-front war at Wittenberg, with Catholics on one front and radicals on the other. It was not Luther's intent to break with Rome when he posted the Ninety-five Theses. Luther would have agreed with Giles of Viterbo, who said in his inaugural sermon at the Fifth Lateran Council of 1512, "Men must be changed by religion, not religion by men."[68]

Luther did, however, react strongly to questionable preaching. He reacted against men like Tetzel, who preached an especially bad theol-ogy of indulgences. And he reacted against a booklet called the *In-structio summaria,* prepared by Albrecht of Magdeburg, which outlined the four graces granted by Pope Leo X in his indulgence bull. The

---

67. Rupp and Drewery, *Martin Luther,* p. 141.

68. Hubert Jedin, *A History of the Council of Trent* (St. Louis, 1957) 1:169.

fourth point in the booklet set down the conditions for gaining indulgences for the dead:

> It is . . . not necessary that the persons who place their contributions in the chest for the dead should be contrite in heart and have orally confessed, since this grace is based simply on the stage of grace in which the dead departed. . . ."[69]

Thesis twenty-seven of the Ninety-five Theses dealt with the famous "Sobald das Geld in Kasten klingt/Die Seele aus dem Fedefeuer springt." ("When the coin in the coffer rings/The soul from purgatory springs.") Luther sent a copy of the 1517 theses to Albrecht with a letter requesting the Archbishop to withdraw his *Instructio* and restrict the indulgence preachers. A Jesuit historian has recently commented:

> On the eve of All Hallows, 1517, therefore, Martin Luther was neither a heretic nor a schismatic; on the contrary, he was a concerned university professor who felt himself 'a monk and a true son of the Church.'[70]

One can credit Luther's orthodoxy for the fact that the papal document *Exsurge Domine*—drawn up to condemn Luther's teaching—was generally off the mark. In fact, this bull of 15 June 1520 was vague in *extremis.* Of the forty-one quotations taken from Luther, no less than twelve did not accurately quote him or correctly express his views. The bull did, however, sharpen the debate by its careless assessment of Luther.[71] After 1520, because of his three famous treatises of that year, Luther's use of Scripture became clear to Rome.

Puritans at Wittenberg

Soon after the 1521 encounter with Charles V, Luther dropped from public view at the Wartburg Castle. From his "Patmos," as he called the self-imposed exile, Luther translated the New Testament into German. At the same time, Luther fretted while fanatics inflamed Wittenberg.

---

69. Hans J. Hillerbrand, *The Reformation* (New York: 1964), p. 41.

70. Robert E. McNally, "The Ninety-five Theses of Martin Luther: 1517-1967," *Theological Studies* 28 (1967):463.

71. Hans J. hIllerbrand, "Martin Luther and the Bull Exsurge Domine," *Theological Studies* 30 (1969):111–12.

On December 19, Andrew Carlstadt announced that on New Year's Day 1522 he would celebrate the Eucharist in both kinds. On Christmas Day 1521 he and Gabriel Zwilling, a monk at Wittenberg, showed up to demand abolition of all masses, images, and church music. On 27 December the famous Zwickau prophets—men like Nicholas Storch and Mark Stübner—appeared. They spoke of visions, dreams, and divine colloquies with God through the Spirit. Stübner described his startling vision of St. John Chrysostom in hell[72] while Carlstadt expounded the prophecies of Malachi and Zechariah.

Luther reappeared in Wittenberg and on 9 March 1522 mounted his pulpit in a monk's garb. This series of sermons showed Luther's dependance on the Word, and the difference between a Reformer and fanatic—a sense of timing. It would be too simple to say Luther used the Word to challenge the fanatics' appeal to Spirit. It was the doctrine of the Word which focused attention on radical obedience.

"It brings Satan distress," claimed Luther, "when we only spread the Word, and let it alone do the work. . . ."[73] Luther concluded, "Outward things can do no harm to faith if only the heart does not put its trust in them. The Word must first capture the hearts of men and then enlighten them; we cannot do it."[74]

Thomas Müntzer (c. 1489-1525)

Many Marxist historians have declared Thomas Müntzer to be the hero of the Peasant Rebellion. According to their view, Luther was the apostle of bourgeois reaction. From Frederick Engels' *Peasant War* to Ernst Bloch's philosophical works, Luther emerges as a betrayer of prophetic justice.[75]

A significant debate over biblical interpretation arose in the encounter between Müntzer and Luther. Müntzer was an accomplished

---

72. Gordon Rupp, *Patterns of Reformation,* p. 113.

73. Gordon Rupp, "Luther and the Puritans," *Luther Today* (Decorah: Luther College Press, 1957), p. 119.

74. Ibid., p. 119.

75. See Abraham Friesen, *Reformation and Utopia: The Marxist Interpretation of the Reformation and its Antecedents* (Wiesbaden: Franz Steiner Verlag, 1974).

Hebraist, good Latinist, and—like Luther—wrote a German Mass. His most famous sermon was his appeal before the Saxon princes of 1524. At that time, Müntzer urged the princes to take the sword and wipe out the godless, because Christ said in Luke 19:27, "Take my enemies and slay them before my eyes."

> The Word must come down from God into our stupified heart and he who is not receptive to the inner Word in the abyss of his soul knows nothing of God though he may have swallowed one hundred thousand bibles.[76]

However, a series of Prague theses did nothing to stir the authorities. The peasants alone seemed prepared in 1523-24 to listen to the angry young mystic who at Allstedt preached a prophetic faith. His was a needed critique of evangelical Protestantism, which for over four hundred years had known little of atonement or suffering for Christ's sake. There was no appeal to visions of the Spirit in Müntzer's sermons, nor was there blasphemy or idolatry. Müntzer's theology was Christocentric and grounded in the Bible, as the following comment reflects:

> O Elect One, read Matt. 16 and you will see that none comes to Faith in Christ unless he first become like him. Then he sees that no outward witness can give him a new nature, and so he looks not to the words of men, but to divine Revelation. He has to break through all manner of Unbelief, Despair and manifold contradictions, indeed must first suffer hell itself. The reprobate simply hugs the Scripture—he is only too ready to believe that Christ has done all his suffering for him. But he will not behold the Lamb of God who opens the Book—for he will not let go of his own soul, or become conformed to the Lamb of God.[77]

Luther rejected Müntzer's appeal to the sword, but there is something poignant about Müntzer's use of the mystical language of abandonment and temptation. Müntzer spoke in accents familiar to Luther when he wrote:

> Like those of old, then, we are affrighted when God wants to make us divine through the Incarnation of his Son, and our Faith is tried as gold in the Furnance [sic]. Yet this is the true King-

---

76. Roland Bainton, *The Age of the Reformation* (Princeton: D. Van Nostrand Company, 1956), p. 116.

77. Rupp, *Patterns of Reformation,* pp. 193–94.

dom of David where Christ rules from his Tree—there the power of the Most High is displayed through the Impossible Work of God in our suffering through the overshadowing of the Holy Ghost—this, then, is the sum of it, that God will give us true Christian Faith through the Incarnation of Christ and our conformity with him in suffering and in life, through the working of the Holy Ghost. This is the Holy Covenant which God swore to Abraham to give us. But this Faith is so rare that it comes only through Temptation—to which may Christ help us all, Amen.[78]

And so master and pupil argued over the meaning of Scripture in sixteenth-century Saxony. Luther's great sermon *Against The Heavenly Prophets* of 1525 smothered Müntzer's wounded cry for social justice. The *Wittenberg Bible* turned the radicals against Luther when it contradicted their appeal to the simple gospel of inspired laymen. Müntzer condemned the "crackbrained easygoing swine of Wittenberg who are scared by the hurricane of roaring waters and the great floods of divine wisdom."[79] Luther in turn said he would not believe Müntzer even if he "swallowed the Holy Ghost, feathers and all." Luther's text seemed to be I Corinthians 11:19 where Paul says, "For there must be factions among you in order that those who have stood the test among you may be recognized." "Christ finds," said Luther, "not only Caiphas among his enemies, but also Judas among his friends."[80]

In any event, the clear lesson is that Luther found the gospel within the Bible. His battle was over the nature of the gospel, not the authority of the Bible. In fact, all parties in the controversy appealed to the Bible; Catholic as well as radical interpreted the text as authority for their point of view. Catholic appeal to salvation and the radical search for suffering show that interpretation of the text was as crucial as its authority. It reminds us that everywhere in the sixteenth century heresy broke out in appeal after appeal to Scripture. But the burning of books, Bibles, and authors could not quench the Spirit of liberty—even theologians could not chain the Word of God. In the end Luther concluded: "I have done nothing but preach, teach and advance the Word of God. While I was with my Philip and my Amsdorf—the Word did its work!"

---

78. Ibid., p. 220.

79. Rupp, "Luther and the Puritans," p. 142.

80. Rupp and Drewery, *Martin Luther,* p. 114.

3 | Reformed Clarity and Certainty

In the autumn of 1557, John Knox attacked the rule of women. No woman had ruled England since Queen Mathilda in the twelfth century. Now the Catholic Queen Mary of England and the Scottish Queen Mary of Guise were objects of Knox's wrath. *The First Blast of the Trumpet against the Monstrous Regiment of Women* is one extreme of the Reformed appeal to the certainty and clarity of Scripture. Knox asked, Did not St. Paul admonish men to beware of woman, particularly of the charms of their hair? For some reason, Knox had more use for Jezebel than for Deborah as a pattern for political comment. It was an embarrassment to see Elizabeth succeed to the English throne in 1558.

John Knox interviewed Mary Queen of Scots on her return from France. Mary asked Knox what right he, a mere subject, had to question God's choice of her as ruler. Knox retorted that as a subject of the realm he had every right. Queen Mary shot back that if God requires subjects to obey their princes, could Knox receive any other religion than hers? "Why do you, John Knox, call Rome a harlot and subvert the Catholic faith?" Mary then asked the classic question: "Ye interpret the Scriptures in one manner, and they interpret in another. Whom shall I believe? And who shall be judge?" John Knox answered the red-haired Stuart queen in September of 1561:

Ye shall believe God that plainly speaketh in his word: and further than the word teaches you, ye neither shall believe the one or the other. The word of God is plain in the self; and if there appear any obscurity in one place, the Holy Ghost, which is never contrarious to himself, explains the same more clearly in other places: so there can remain no doubt but unto such as obstinately remain ignorant.[1]

A second example of Reformed concern for Scripture may be seen in Zurich, where on 29 January 1523 Ulrich Zwingli held a public debate. The Catholic representatives were surprised that the public audience numbered six hundred with the council in attendance. The evangelical preachers had Great Bibles open before them in Latin, Hebrew, and Greek. When John Faber cried, "There must be a judge," Zwingli shot back, "The Spirit of God out of Holy Scripture itself is the judge."[2]

Zwingli wrote a treatise with the title *Of The Clarity and Certainty of the Word of God.* There Zwingli mused over God's teaching:[3]

Again, I know for certain that God teaches me, because I have experienced the fact of it. . . . When I was younger, I gave myself overmuch to human teaching, like others of my day. . . . But eventually I came to the point where led by the Word and Spirit of God I saw the need to set aside all these things and to learn the doctrine of God direct from his own Word. Then I began to ask God for light and the Scriptures became far clearer to me—even though I read nothing else—than if I had studied many commentators and expositors.

Those in the Reformed tradition—Zwingli, Bullinger, Bucer, Calvin, Beza, Martyr, Musculus, and Knox—all share in this concern for the clarity of the Word and certainty of the Spirit. But despite the claim to certainty, these Reformed theologians often could not convince their Lutheran or Catholic friends that certain passages of Scripture were all that clear. Zwingli's 1529 dispute over John 6 with Luther at Marburg

---

1. John Knox, *History of the Reformation in Scotland* ed. William Croft Dickinson (New York: Philosophical Library, 1950), 2:18.

2. Gordon Rupp, "The Swiss Reformers and the Sects," *The New Cambridge Modern History: The Reformation 1520-59* (Cambridge: At the University Press) 2:101.

3. *Zwingli And Bullinger,* ed. G. W. Bromiley (Philadelphia: The Westminster Press, 1953), pp. 90–91.

and dissent over the plain meaning of Romans 13 reflects the negative side of this Scripture principle.

COMMENTARY

The Bible was used in many ways to educate folk during the Reformation. In the cultural context of sixteenth century humanism, every baptized person was encouraged to read his own Bible, hymnbook, and catechism.[4] Melanchthon's *School Regulations* of 1528 influenced several patterns of instruction in which biblical texts were used. The technique of memorization was supported in the classic treatise of John Sturm at Strasbourg, the *De literarum ludis recte aperiendis* of 1538. At Strasbourg the Protestant Academy fostered such study. John Sturm wrote that it was vital to "maintain in our Schools of Theology Moses, the prophets, the evangelists, the apostles, and, in order to explain them, the authority of the fathers. . . . Therefore let us fight for religion and for letters. . . ."[5]

One of the more popular subjects was biblical history in the form of school plays. Sebastian Castellio, in his *Sacred Dialogues* (which went through more than a hundred editions), gave an account of Paul's trial before Ananias based on Acts 23:

> *Paul:* Men, brothers—up till the present time, I have always served God with a good conscience.
> *Ananias:* Somebody, hit him in the mouth!
> *Paul:* God will hit you, you painted wall! How can you dare to judge me by the Law, and command that I be struck, contrary to the Law:
> *Attendant:* Do you dare to shout at the high priest of God?
> *Paul:* Brethren, I didn't know that this was the high priest. Yes, it's written in Scripture, 'Thou shalt not revile the ruler of thy people.' Now listen to the truth, brothers present in this assembly. I am a Pharisee, and the son of a Pharisee. The charge against me is that I hope in the resurrection of the dead.

4. Lowell Green, "The Bible in Sixteenth-Century Humanist Education," *Studies In The Renaissance* 19 (1972):118–20.

5. Pierre Mesnard, "The Pedagogy of Johann Sturm (1507-1589) and its Evangelical Inspiration," *Studies In The Renaissance* 13 (1966):214 n.8.

Sadducee: The clever rascal! He hopes to get out of it that way.

Pharisee: He has spoken well; I see nothing wrong in him. Perhaps a spirit or an angel [genius] has spoken to him. Let's not fight against God!

Sadducee: You're defending yourselves now, because he claims to agree with you!

Pharisee: We're defending him, because he deserves our defense. What's he really done wrong? Do you want to attack the innocent?

Sadducee: It's really the other way around—do you want to protect the guilty?

Lysias: Something's got to be done, or this man'll be pulled apart. You! Command the army to go down there, and bring him up into the castle![6]

Ulrich Zwingli (1484-1531)

In 1518, the Zurich authorities invited Zwingli to become the secular priest of the Great Church. On New Year's Day, 1519, his thirty-fifth birthday, Zwingli startled his congregation with an announcement that he would abandon the appointed scriptural readings and preach straight through the Gospel of St. Matthew. This new mode of preaching brought the Reformation to Zurich by 1525.

In September 1519 Zwingli fell dangerously ill at a time when nearly a third of the city died of the plague. He set down in song his new faith in Christ while recovering from near death.

> And if Thou yet
>   Wouldst have me dead,
> Amidst my earthly days,
>   Yet may I still Thee praise.
> Thy will be done!
>   Nought can me stun.
> Thy tool to make
>   I am, or break![7]

As his preaching became mature, Zwingli often revealed a sense of humor in his translations. In fact, the twenty-third psalm came out with the following expression:

---

6. Green, "The Bible in Sixteenth-Century Humanist Education," p. 127.

7. Oscar Farner, *Zwingli the Reformer* (New York: Philosophical Library, 1952), p. 35.

> The Lord is my shepherd,
>   I shall not want
> He makes me rest
>   in lovely Alpine pastures.[8]

Myconius, Zwingli's biographer, relates that Zwingli memorized the Pauline epistles in Greek. His faith in the Word of God never slackened over twelve years of preaching. He explained, "God now sends His Word, that it may heal.... The Word of God will take its course as surely as does the Rhine—one may dam it up for a while but cannot stop its flow!"[9] At Zurich this new form of preaching led to innovations in worship, the abolition of church music, and the practice known as prophesying.

On Maundy Thursday, 1525, Zwingli celebrated the Lord's Supper at a simple table, over which was spread a linen cloth and plain vessels of wood. Zwingli prayed in German with his face to the congregation, and gave both bread and wine to the people. Then he prayed the 133rd psalm and sent the people away with the words, "Go in peace."

"The Prophecy" at Zurich began in June 1525, perhaps in obedience to I Corinthians 14:26-33, "Let everything be done in decency and in order" (1525 was also the year of extreme Anabaptist opposition in Zurich). Every day at seven a.m. except Sunday and Friday, students and pastors gathered in the Cathedral. One person read the text for the day in Latin, another gave the Hebrew, while a third reader gave aloud the Greek of the Septuagint and explained the passage. A fourth described in Latin how one should preach on the passage while another, sometimes Zwingli himself, would preach (in German) on the carefully studied text. This not only aided the students assembled but eventually resulted in the Zurich translation of the Bible.

In 1576 Edmund Grindal, Archbishop of Canterbury, fell into a serious disagreement with his sovereign Queen Elizabeth. Elizabeth objected to the now-widespread religious exercise called "prophesyings." This had developed over the years, and provided training for the clergy and edification for the laity. The prophesyings got their name from

---

8. Ibid., p. 66.

9. Ibid., p. 41.

I Corinthians 14:29, where Paul wrote, "Let the prophets speak two or three, and let the other judge."

The prophesyings were conducted in a variety of ways. Bishop Gheast (who reported no exercises in his diocese of Salisbury, due to the lack of learned moderators) had heard of three different ways of proceeding:

> In one dioceise a text of Scripture is chosen to be entreated of, and certeyn be appoynted to shewe there myndes of it and the rest be hearers. And in an other dioceise a common place is handled by some appoynted to speake thereof. And in the thyrd dioceise a common place is taken out of Musculus or of Calvine and everie minister is commanded to speake his mynde of the said place.

John Mullins, Archdeacon of London, reported that he conducted exercises twice each year for periods of four or five days. He ordered the clergymen who were not qualified preachers to study several chapters of Scripture privately and at each meeting, he examined the clergymen on the meaning of the passages. In this fashion the Archdeacon covered most of the New Testament during his fifteen years in office.

Although some bishops (and the queen) were critical of the exercise as a possible platform for radical ideas, by and large, the bishops were for their continuance if properly handled. The argument given in favor of the exercise was their great profit to poorly educated ministers. Another reason given was that it kept the clergy out of mischief. Bishop Berkeley stated, "They would compell men to study and kepe them from idelness and from vunlawfule games."

Bishop Curtis stated that the exercises served to "stage the ministers from gaminge, from drinckyne, from wanderinge vpe and doune from towne to towne, from markettes to markettes, and from fayre to fayre." The lay people also greatly appreciated these exercises and often would come from miles around to listen in on what was being said.[10] In the end Grindal told Elizabeth, "Remember Madam, you are mortal"; Elizabeth reminded the Archbishop that she was Queen—by urging Grindal's resignation.

---

10. Above account taken from Stanford E. Lehmberg, "Archbishop Grindal and the Prophesyings," *Historical Magazine of the Protestant Episcopal Church* 34 (1965):87–145.

From Switzerland to Salisbury, the literal understanding of I Corinthians 14:29 effected a biblical Reformation. In Switzerland this Reformation was caused also by academic disputation based on the knowledge of Greek and Hebrew and of patristic literature. In the political center of the Swiss Confederacy, Berne, Lutheran doctrine was banned in 1523, but scriptural preaching was permitted. By 1525 Berthold Haller at Berne had even substituted preaching for the Roman Mass and in 1527 had gained sufficient control (via the Reformed party) to set a debate for 6 January 1528. Haller drew up ten theses—which Zwingli edited.

Three hundred and fifty ecclesiastics gathered at Berne from several Swiss cantons and South German cities. Joachim von Watt of St. Gall presided over the twenty-day discussion. All ten theses were signed by the cantons and ministers of Berne. Thesis one sums up their concern for the Word of God: "The holy, Christian Church, whose only Head is Christ, is born of the Word of God, abides in the same, and does not listen to the voice of strangers."[11] The Bernese Council voted for reform after hearing the debate.

During the second Kappel war, Ulrich Zwingli died on the battlefield. He wrote in his will:

> May God send his thunder and hail upon us if we allow the Holy Scriptures to be distorted. Take care that the divine Word is loyally proclaimed amongst you. . . . Listen to the Word of God! That alone will set you right again.[12]

And so we see that Zurich commentary on Scripture ran the gamut from sermon to prophesy, from the Zurich Bible to controversy with Catholics, Anabaptists, and Lutherans. And it left its impact on Elizabethan England with the Puritan prophesyings.

Heinrich Bullinger (1503-1575)

Zwingli's death left the young scholar Heinrich Bullinger in charge of biblical reform at Zurich, where he remained for the next forty years.

---

11. Arthur C. Cochrane, *Reformed Confessions of the Sixteenth Century* (Philadelphia: Westminster Press, 1966), p. 49.

12. Farner, *Zwingli the Reformer,* p. 135.

Bullinger is better known as the author of the *Second Hevetic Confession* (1566) than as a biblical commentator, though careful study reveals his impact on Reformed theologians such as John Calvin and Peter Martyr. Bullinger was forced to flee to Zurich after the 1531 Protestant defeat at Kappel. Shortly after his arrival, Zurich chose Bullinger to succeed Zwingli. From his first sermon on 9 December 1531 until 1542, Bullinger preached six to eight times a week. A set of fifty sermons known as the *Decades* were published in English, and through them Bullinger left his mark on Tudor England. Without Zwingli the Zurich Reformation would have been difficult; without Bullinger it would not have lasted.

In his diary Bullinger described the delight which Melanchthon's *Loci Communes* gave him during 1521-22. Then, between 1525 and 1527 Bullinger himself commented on all the Pauline epistles and Hebrews. Each of his manuscript lectures began with an historical introduction, included a summary at the head of each chapter, followed by a verse-by-verse exegesis and a paraphrase. Each chapter ended with a list of notable topics.[13]

Bullinger composed a 1527 letter on method which analyzed the study of sacred Scripture. "Because Holy Scripture is from God, it can only be understood by a heart devoted to God, by a mind purged from all stains, by a life free from all impurity."[14]

Bullinger insisted that a student must first of all master the languages, particularly Greek and Hebrew. Then he must understand the intent, or scope, of Scripture—which he defined as the covenant between God and man. According to Bullinger, in a reasonable approach to Scripture attention should be directed to the context, circumstance, and relationship of the text to other biblical passages. The status or chief subject under discussion must also not be neglected.[15] In the preface to his lecture on the Pauline epistles, Bullinger sets forth his triple plan of exposition: brevity; faithfulness to the text; and attention to every facet of the argument.

---

13. T.H.L. Parker, *Calvin's New Testament Commentaries* (Grand Rapids: Eerdmans, 1971), p. 38.

14. Ibid., p. 39.

15. Ibid., pp. 39–40.

Two of Bullinger's works comment further on Scripture. Miles Coverdale translated one of these, called *The Old Faith and True Religion,* in 1547. Chapter six of this book interpreted God's law given to Moses as one which leads to Christ. But Bullinger's hearers complained that "Here is nothing heard of faith, but much, yea only of works."[16] Bullinger answered that Paul's words in Galatians 3 give one the proper understanding of testament or covenant: "God gave it freely unto Abraham by promise."[17] Similar to Lutheran exegesis which followed a law/gospel motif, Reformed expositors like Bullinger saw a pattern of promise/fulfillment. These models for extracting the meaning from Scripture join the various methods outlined by the commentators. Both theological models and philological methods are part of biblical study in the Reformation period.

Bullinger, in sermon three of the *Fifth Decade*, describes his concern for a ministry of the Word: "For this cause ministers are called saviours: They are said to convert men: their word is called, not the word of man, but the word of God. . . ."[18] He added, "The apostles are preachers and ministers of the gospel, not of the letter, but of the Spirit. . . ."[19]

John Calvin (1509-1564)

Calvin's commentaries are models for his time. There and in sermon after sermon the Genevan Reformer related biblical text to its context as he commented on most of scripture. Much work needs to be done on the pattern of Calvin's exegesis, which is now carefully outlined in T.H.L. Parker's masterful survey of the New Testament commentaries. Other considerations must be noted, however. First, Calvin's doctrine of Scripture is in dispute; second, many of his sermons are being re-

---

16. *Writings and Translations of Myles Coverdale, Bishop of Exeter* (Cambridge: At The University Press, 1844), p. 41.

17. Ibid., p. 42.

18. *The Decades of Henry Bullinger* (Cambridge: At The University Press, 1852), p. 95.

19. Ibid., p. 100.

covered and edited for the first time in the twentieth century. Calvin's commentaries and sermons inevitably lead us to the famous *Institutes.*

Just as John Warwick Montgomery argues for Luther, J. I. Packer and Kenneth Kantzer claim that John Calvin was an authority for inerrancy of the biblical text. Kantzer links Calvin's doctrine of the knowledge of God to that of Scripture: "The merest glance at Calvin's commentaries will demonstrate how seriously the reformer applied his rigid doctrine of verbal inerrancy to his exegesis of scripture."[20]

Calvin's appeal to the internal witness of the Spirit in the *Institutes* 1.8 is not, in Kantzer's view, a validation of the external revelation in Scripture:[21]

> Calvin stands unequivocally for the view that the entire body of written Scriptures was dictated by the Spirit of God. His teaching is so clear and he reiterates his point so frequently, no other conclusion is possible.[22]

Infallible, unerring rule, steadfast decree—all these terms are found in Calvin. And, it is true that Calvin uses the term *dictation,* which does require elucidation. But must we add *inerrancy* to the list of synonyms for saving doctrine?

James Packer turns to Calvin's definition of biblical inspiration given in the comments on II Timothy 3:16. Packer interprets this passage in Calvin to mean that the text of the Bible is the same as the doctrine dictated by the Holy Ghost.[23] Packer concludes:

> All Scripture has the same double aspect: it consists of words of men which are also words of God and so is to be received, every particle of it, as having proceeded from God's very mouth.[24]

---

20. Kenneth S. Kantzer, "Calvin and the Holy Scriptures," ed. John F. Walvoord, *Inspiration and Interpretation* (Grand Rapids: Eerdmans, 1957) p. 142. See also Richard C. Prust, "Was Calvin a Biblical Literalist?" *Scottish Journal of Theology* 20 (1967): 312–28.

21. Kantzer, "Calvin and the Holy Scriptures," p. 129.

22. Ibid., pp. 138–139.

23. J. I. Packer, "Calvin's view of Scripture," ed. John W. Montgomery, *God's Inerrant Word* (Minneapolis: Bethany Fellowship, 1974), pp. 102–103.

24. Ibid., p. 104.

Ex dono ... ponex ... En ...

CHRISTIA

NAE RELIGIONIS INSTI-
tutio, totam ferè pietatis summã, & quic
quid est in doctrina salutis cognitu ne=
cessariui, complectens: omnibus pie=
tatis studiosis lectu dignissi=
mum opus, ac re .....
cens edi=
tum.

M (VDanning

Maij ... 1634

PRAEFATIO AD CHRI
stianißimum REGEM FRANCIAE, *qua*
hic ei liber pro confeßione fidei
offertur.

IOANNE CALVINO
Nouiodunensi autore.

BASILEAE,
M. D. XXXVI.

Title page to the first edition of John Calvin's **Institutes**. Printed at Basel by
Thomas Platter and Balthasar Lasius in March of 1536.

Some modern scholars claim that Calvin's view of inspiration included inerrancy, and that Reformation Geneva is one of the major battlefields in the modern battle over the Bible. That may have been true in the seventeenth century, but we are talking about an entirely different war over Word and Spirit, or Scripture and Papacy. Calvin defines doctrine in his comments on II Timothy 3:16:

> In order to uphold the authority of the Scripture, he declares that it is divinely inspired; for, if it be so, it is beyond all controversy that men ought to receive it with reverence. This is a principle which distinguishes our religion from all others, that we know that God hath spoken to us, and are fully convinced that the prophets did not speak at their own suggestion, but that, being organs of the Holy Spirit, they only uttered what they had been commissioned from heaven to declare. Whoever then wishes to profit in the Scriptures, let him, first of all, lay down this as a settled point, that the Law and the Prophets are not a doctrine delivered according to the will and pleasure of men, but dictated by the Holy Spirit.[25]

The meaning of "doctrine . . . dictated by the Holy Spirit" needs further attention. Kantzer and Packer identify doctrine with the text of the Bible, but Calvin's words hold another meaning. In the *Institutes* Calvin says "all right knowledge of God is born of obedience."[26] According to Calvin, the Scriptures *contain* a doctrine dictated by the Spirit which awaits the same Spirit's witness, i.e. obedience to the preached Word. God is author of the doctrine: man is author of the text. In the *Institutes* 1.7.4 Calvin argues that the Spirit seals Scripture:

> For as God alone can properly bear witness to his own words, so these words will not obtain full credit in the hearts of men, until they are sealed by the inward testimony of the Spirit.

In the *Institutes* 1.8.13 Calvin concludes:

> Then only, therefore, does Scripture suffice to give a saving knowledge of God when its certainty is founded on the inward persuasion of the Holy Spirit.

---

25. John Calvin, *Commentaries on the Epistles to Timothy, Titus and Philemon* (Grand Rapids: Eerdmans, 1948), pp. 248–49. See Hans-Joachim Kraus, "Calvin's Exegetical Principles," *Interpretation* 31 (1977):10.

26. *Institutes* I. 6.2. That experience surpasses reason. See Charles Portee, *Calvin and Classical Philosophy* (Leiden: E. J. Brill, 1977), pp. 36–41.

Bullinger's *Second Helvetic Confession* defines this process further in the section called "The Preaching of the Word of God is the Word of God."[27] Inward illumination requires external preaching, and true interpretation is never a private opinion (II Peter 1:20). Bullinger's 1566 confession is pertinent to the kind of authority these Reformed scholars found in Scripture:

> But we hold that interpretation of the Scripture to be orthodox and genuine which is gleaned from the Scriptures themselves (from the nature of the language in which they were written, likewise according to the circumstances in which they were set down, and expounded in the light of like and unlike passages and of many and clearer passages) and which agree with the rule of faith and love and contributes much to the glory of God and man's salvation.[28]

Zwingli, Calvin, Bullinger, and Peter Martyr (who helped Bullinger with the *Second Helvetic Confession)* gave primary concern to the truth of doctrine in Scripture, which the Holy Spirit sealed inwardly and a legitimate ministry preached outwardly. They did not consider doctrine identical with the text of Scripture, nor did they claim that the Spirit bore witness to an inner feeling. Instead, external preaching according to the rule of faith and love was regarded as the very Word of God.

But, since that preaching led our scholars to burn heretics at the stake, obviously their view of Scripture as clear and certain calls for further explanation. The application of their rule of faith and love violated the clear intent of other Scripture passages such as Matthew 5 in which Christ urged his true followers to pray for their persecutors. What kind of perverted logic would use certain texts to run roughshod over the ideas and bodies of men for whom Christ died in love? Sadly, the men of the Reformation abandoned humane aspects of Christian conduct in favor of logical rigor. And their successors do not seem to have learned the lesson from history when they confuse inerrancy and infallibility.

Calvin preached regularly in Geneva, having gained valuable practice during three years in Strasbourg with Martin Bucer. From 1549-1564,

---

27. Cochrane, *Reformed Confessions of the Sixteenth Century,* p. 225.

28. Ibid., p. 226.

Dennis Raguenier recorded these sermons in shorthand. 870 sermons
were published in the 1863-1900 edition of Calvin's works known as
the *Corpus Reformatorum*. At least forty-four volumes of sermons tran-
scribed by Raguenier were sold by the Geneva University Library in
1805. By 1887 fourteen manuscript copies had been returned (including one not owned by the University Library in 1805), and the Bodleian at Oxford owned another. In 1963 Lambeth Palace Library in
London purchased a previously unknown set of sermons on Genesis
1-4. An international project is now underway to publish these sermons
that modern scholarship has not yet tapped.[29]

T.H.L. Parker asks the reader who smiles at such pulpit "nostalgia"
whether he would prefer

> to listen to the secondhand views on a religion of social ethics, or
> the ill-digested piety, delivered in slipshod English, that he will
> hear today in most churches . . . or three hundred and forty-two
> sermons on the Book of the Prophet Isaiah, sermons born of an
> infinite passion of faith and a burning sincerity, sermons lumi-
> nous with theological sense, lively with wit and imagery, showing
> depths of compassion and the unquenchable joyousness of
> hope.

Calvin preached without notes direct from his Hebrew Old Testament
and Greek New Testament. In his expositions he took a clause from its
biblical context and applied it directly to the needs of the people.
Parker has translated Calvin's explanation as follows:

> As often as we come to the sermon we are taught of the free
> promises of God, to show us that it is in his pure goodness and
> mercy that we must entirely repose, that we must not be ground-
> ed on our own merits or anything that we can bring on our side,
> but that God must hold out his hand to us, to commence and
> accomplish all. And this (as Scripture shows us) is applied to us
> by our Lord Jesus Christ; and that in such a way that we must
> seek him entirely . . . and that Jesus Christ alone must be our
> advocate. That, I say, is shewn us every day.[30]

---

29. T.H.L. Parker, "Calvini Opera Sed Non Omnia," *Scottish Journal of Theology* 18 (1965):194–203.

30. T.H.L. Parker, *John Calvin: A Biography,* (London: J.M. Dent & Sons,
1975), p. 92, 94.

One sample of Calvin's sermons must suffice as an example of Calvin's Geneva preaching. In sermon three, Calvin comments on Psalm 84:

> We have our eyes bente to this ende, to knowe God better and better. Here there are two things requisite: one is that we be diligent to frequent sermons, and publique praiers. The second is, that we knowe wherefore wee frequent them.... To what end therefore do we assemble our/selves? Wherefore is the Gospell preached unto us? ... unlesse it be that God may be magnified in us? Nowe this praise consisteth not onely in the tip of the tongue ... but it strecheth out it selfe thorowe our whole life.[31]

From prophecy to preaching the Reformed theologians confronted secular men with sacred doctrine. The text was the means through which doctrine was preached and through which the Spirit sealed the elect whom God alone had chosen. When once we understand that for Calvin preaching was the very Word of God, we can turn to his 1540 Romans commentary with greater appreciation. (An account of Reformation Romans commentaries is long overdue. Humanists such as Erasmus, and reforming cardinals such as Sadoleto, Contrarini, and Seripando—as well as Luther, Calvin, and their associates—all published expositions of this Pauline letter.[32])

Calvin's commentary is a fruit of his Strasbourg pastorate of 1538-41 with Martin Bucer, who was himself a diligent expositor of Romans. Calvin's 1536-37 lectures at Geneva paved the way for his preface, which speaks about "lucid brevity" and the plan to improve the quality of exposition. Wendelin Rihel published Calvin's Romans in March 1540 with some copies carrying a pseudonym on the second title page: *The Commentaries of Alciun on Paul's Epistle to the Romans.*[33]

There have been exciting discoveries of the French versions of the *Argument to Romans:* T.H.L. Parker located a 1545 French *Argument et Sommaire* and Rudolphe Peter of Strasbourg came across the 1543

---

31. John Calvin, *Foure Sermons... with a briefe expositon of the LXXXVII. Psalme. Translated... by John Fielde* (London: Thomas Man, 1579), pp. 36, 39.

32. See John B. Payne, "Erasmus and Lefevre d'Etaples as Interpreters of Paul," *Archiv für Reformationsgeschichte* 65 (1974):54–82. Also/see my "Peter Martyr on Romans," *Scottish Journal of Theology* 26 (1973):401–20.

33. T.H.L. Parker, *John Calvin: A Biography,* p. 74.

version in Geneva (according to Peter, a second copy of the entire *Argument* exists in Bordeaux). The whole commentary appeared in French translation in 1550 at Geneva.

The form of Calvin's Romans commentary set the pattern for his future commentaries. In chapters 1—5 Calvin taught that "man's only righteousness is through the mercy of God in Christ, which being offered by the Gospel is apprehended by faith." Since men sleep in their sin and delude themselves about self-righteousness, Paul proceeded to do two things—"to convince men of iniquity, and to shake off the torpor of those whom he proves guilty."[34]

The commentary divides chapters of Romans into sections, with Calvin's own literal Latin translation at the head. Calvin selected Colines' Greek text (published in Paris, 1534), which was based on readings of many manuscripts not used in any other sixteenth-century printed Greek Testament. Calvin's commentaries are therefore based on a sounder text than any other contemporary Greek Testament would have provided. In Romans 1-5 there are twenty-five variant readings, twenty-one are significant, and of those Calvin agrees with Colines seventeen times.[35]

Calvin's exegesis and exposition relied on Bude, Erasmus, Chrysostom, Josephus, Pliny, and other dependable sources. However, Parker warns:

> To say that he let the text speak to him would be trite and misleading. Rather, he conducted a continual enquiry between the detail and the wider context. . . . As he listened to the context he questioned the immediate text; as he listened to the immediate text he questioned the context. It was by this continual process of hearing and of asking . . . that Calvin was able to arrive in the remarkable way that he did at the 'mind' of the author.[36]

---

34. John Calvin, *Commentaries on the Epistle of Paul the Apostle to the Romans* (Grand Rapids: Eerdmans, 1948), pp. 29–30.

35. T.H.L. Parker, *Calvin's New Testament Commentaries,* pp. 106–109.

36. T.H.L. Parker, *John Calvin: A Biography,* p. 76. See also the fine survey by John H. Leith, "John Calvin—Theologian of the Bible," *Interpretation* 25 (1971):329–44. Cf. R. A. Hassler, "Influence of David and the Psalms upon John Calvin's Life and Thought," *Hartford Seminary Quarterly* 5 (1965):7–18.

Calvin's Romans of 1540 deserves careful reading. One article on the 1540 Romans concludes, in fact, that the doctrinal subject of justification in the 1539 *Institutes* is "the main hinge on which all religion turns."[37] However, Parker states:

> It would be incorrect to speak of Calvin conceiving his task of expositor as making the New Testament relevant to his age. He knows that he does not need to, that indeed he cannot make it relevant, for it is, as the Gospel, the living Word of God concerning the living and active Christ.[38]

CONFESSION

When Mary Tudor succeeded the Protestant Edward VI in 1553, several groups of exiles left England for the Continent. The struggle between Knox and Cox over the 1552 Prayer Book at Frankfort was partly responsible for that exodus. In 1560, the group at Geneva published an English translation known as the *Geneva Bible,* whose preface gives a Reformed confession of faith dedicated to Queen Elizabeth. The Geneva translators urged that the work of Christ in England needed "a lively and steadfast faith in Christ Jesus, who must dwell in our hearts as the only means and assurance of our salvation." A second need was "that our faith bring forth good fruits."[39] Then came the brave confession:

> The church of Christ even under the cross hath from the beginning of the world been victorious, and shall be everlasting. Truth it is that sometime it seemeth to be shadowed with a cloud or driven with a stormy persecution yet suddenly the beams of Christ the sun of justice shine and bring it to light and liberty. If for a time it lie covered with ashes, yet it is quickly kindled again by the wind of God's Spirit; though it seem drowned in the sea, or parched and pined in the wilderness yet God giveth ever good success. . . .[40]

---

37. H. Paul Santmire, "Justification in Calvin's 1540 Romans Commentary," *Church History* 33 (1964): 294.

38. T.H.L. Parker, *Calvin's New Testament Commentaries,* p. 92.

39. Leonard J. Trinterud, *Elizabethan Puritanism* (New York: Oxford University Press, 1971), p. 213.

40. Ibid., pp. 213–14.

THE
NEWE TESTAMENT
OF OVR LORD
IESVS CHRIST,

Conferred diligently with the Greke, and beſt appro-
ued tranſlacions in diuers languages.

EXOD. XIIII, VER. XIII.

*FEARE YE NOT, STAND STIL, AND BE-
holde the ſaluacion of the Lord, which he wil ſhewe to you this day.*

Great are the troubles of the righteous:

but the Lord deliuereth them out of all, Pſal. 34. 19.

THE LORD SHAL FIGHT FOR YOV:
therefore holde you your peace, Exod. 14, ver. 14.

AT GENEVA.

PRINTED BY ROVLAND HALL.

M. D. LX.

Geneva Bible New Testament, the earliest English Bible printed in Roman type
with verse divisions. This New Testament is a careful revision of William Witting-
hams's Testament of 1557 compared with Theodore Beza's Latin translation.

Calvin on the Christian Life

The church under the cross, braced by the stiff wind of God's Spirit, confessed its confidence in the Holy Scriptures. As the Berne thesis had said, the Church was born out of the Word of God. Calvin wrote a brief description of the Christian life for his 1539 *Institutes of The Christian Religion.*[41] According to Calvin, the person and redemption of Christ gives the strongest motive for the Christian life. Calvin wrote that one must devote himself to righteousness,[42] for the Christian life is a matter of the heart, rather than the tongue only: "For it is a doctrine not of the tongue but of life. . . . it must enter our heart and pass into our daily living, and so transform us into itself that it may not be unfruitful for us."[43] Each believer is to set this target before him and press toward the goal "with wavering and limping and even creeping along the ground."[44]

In a similar way the *Genevan Confession* of 1536 set forth faith as confidence:

> We confess that the entrance which we have to the great treasures and riches of the goodness of God that is vouch safed to us is by faith; inasmuch as, in certain confidence and assurance of heart, we believe in the promises of the Gospel, and receive Jesus Christ as he is offered to us by the Father and described to us by the Word of God.[45]

The catechism of the church of Geneva had great influence during the sixteenth century. The Puritan party in England adopted the version of Alexander Nowell, Dean of St. Paul's,[46] and the French text divided the catechism into fifty-five sections. In describing the road by which one comes to eternal life Calvin wrote:

---

41. *Institutes* III. VI. 1–5. McNeil edition, pp. 684– 9.

42. Ibid., p. 687.

43. Ibid., p. 688.

44. Ibid., p. 689.

45. John Calvin, *Theological Treatises,* ed. J.K.S. Reid (Philadelphia: Westminster Press, 1954), p. 29.

46. William P. Haugaard, "John Calvin and the Catechism of Alexander Nowell," *Archiv für Reformationsgeschichte* 61 (1970):50–65.

> *Pupil:* To this end God has left us his sacred Word. For spiritual doctrine is a kind of door by which we enter into his celestial Kingdom.
>
> *Master:* Where must we seek this Word?
>
> *Pupil:* In the Holy Scriptures in which it is contained.
>
> *Master:* How should it be used to obtain profit from it?
>
> *Pupil:* If we lay hold on it with complete heartfelt conviction ... if we show ourselves docile to it; if we subdue our wills and minds to his obedience; if we love it heartily. ... —then it will turn to our salvation, as intended.[47]

Clearly Calvin was persuaded that the Word of promise was contained in the Holy Scriptures of Old and New Testament. God's word profited the believer when he obeyed it, said Calvin, for only then did the Spirit confirm His Word for salvation.

Reformed Confessions

We have already mentioned Bullinger's *Second Helvetic Confession* of 1566. This and other Reformed confessions assign several different roles to Scripture. A glimpse at these will show alternate uses of Scripture in the sixteenth century.

In 1530, Strasbourg and three other cities set forth their own confession rather than sign the Lutheran *Augsburg Confession.* This *Tetrapolitan Confession* opens with a chapter on the subject-matter of sermons. At Strasbourg the authorities refused to allow the cathedral pulpit to be used for evangelical preaching. So, the carpenters made a portable wooden pulpit, bore it into the middle of the cathedral each time Matthew Zell preached, and carefully took it back home after every sermon.[48] Naturally, therefore, the *Tetrapolitan* quotes from Paul, that "divinely inspired scripture is profitable for doctrine," and focuses on the task of preaching.[49] We observe that at Berne the con-

---

47. Ibid., pp. 129–30. Note Calvin's "Ubinam quaerendum nobis est hoc verbum? In scripturis sanctis, quibus continetur," in Petrus Barth, ed., *Joannis Calvini Opera Selecta Volumen II* (Monachii: In Aedibus Chr. Kaiser, 1952), p. 128.

48. Mirian Chrisman, *Strasbourg and the Reform* (New Haven: Yale University Press, 1967), p. 100.

49. Cochrane, *Reformed Confessions of the Sixteenth Century,* pp. 55–56.

cern was birth of the church out of Scripture; Bullinger centered on the human task of scriptural exegesis; and the *Tetrapolitan* emphasized preaching which nourishes growth of the church.

The 1560 *Scottish Confession of Faith* contains even a different attitude toward Scripture:

> When controversy arises about the right understanding of any passage or sentence of Scripture ... we ought not so much to ask what men have said or done before us, as what the Holy Ghost uniformly speaks within the body of the Scriptures and what Christ Jesus Himself did and commanded.[50]

According to the *Scottish Confession,* conflict is settled by appeal to the Spirit who in His Word cannot contradict Himself. One compares a difficult text with a plainer text and uses the rule of love.[51]

The Presbyterian *Book of Confessions* and Cochrane's *Reformed Confessions of the Sixteenth Century* leave out the 1549 *Zurich Consensus.* Its Christology starts with Christ as the end of the law, for "knowledge of him comprehends, in itself, the sum total of the gospel."[52] Article IV describes Christ as priest and as king:

> He is also to be reckoned a brother who has made us blessed sons of God who were once miserable sons of Adam. He is also to be reckoned as a repairer who reforms whatever is vicious in us by the virtue of his Spirit, so that we may cease to live after the world and the flesh and so that God himself may abide in us. He must be reckoned as king, who enriches us with every kind of good thing, who rules and protects us by his power, who provides us with spiritual weapons that we may stand unconquered against the world and the devil, who frees us from all harm and who governs and guides us by the sceptre of his mouth.

Along with cathechisms, creeds, and précis of the Christian life, Reformed Christians loved the Psalter. And so our account of confessions would not be complete without a reference to Clement Marot. This French Protestant hymnist completed a metrical version of the

---

50. Ibid., p. 177.

51. Ibid., p. 177.

52. "The *Consensus Tigurinus,*" trans. Ian D. Bunting, *Journal of Presbyterian History* 44 (1966):45 (Article I).

Psalms from Vatable's Latin version. Twelve of these psalms were included in the first Calvinist hymnbook published at Strasbourg in 1539. A Strasbourg refugee from the Low Countries who was moved by the psalm-singing wrote:

> Everyone sings, men and women, and it is a lovely sight. Each has a music book in his hand. . . . For five or six days at the beginning as I looked on this little company of exiles, I wept, not for sadness but for joy to hear them all singing so heartily, and as they sang giving thanks to God that he had led them to a place where his name is glorified. No one could imagine what joy there is in singing the praises and wonders of the Lord in the mother tongue as they are sung here.[53]

Marot at Calvin's urging translated twenty more psalms for the 1542 *Cinquante pseaumes*. In 1562 Theodore Beza completed the hymnbook, adding 101 of his own psalms to Marot's forty-nine. The French metrical psalter was so popular that sixty-two editions were printed in two years, and it appeared in twenty-four languages.

Zwingli at Zurich, however, forbade church music. He endorsed Paul, who urged silent worship and the *inward* "singing of psalms and hymns, spiritual songs, singing with grace in your hearts to the Lord" (Col. 3:16). Zwingli wrote:

> But should it not be good, they say, for one to sing the praise of God before all man. Answer: Show me that it is good and I will believe it to be good. God alone is good and the sole source of all good things [Matt. 19:17; Jer. 2:13]. If the mumbling of psalms is good, then it must come from God. Show me where God has commanded such moaning, mumbling, and murmuring."[54]

Zwingli opposed choral singing in which the text was obscured by the versatility of a performer's voice.

The less rigid Calvin, however, endorsed congregational singing of metrical psalms. Calvin explained in the 1542 Genevan service book that prayer can be spoken and sung:

---

53. Quoted in T.H.L. Parke, *John Calvin: A Biography,* p. 69.

54. Charles Garside, Jr., *Zwingli And The Arts* (New Haven: Yale University Press, 1966), p. 44.

And in truth, we know by experience, that singing has great strength and vigor to move and inflame the heart of men to invoke and praise God with a more vehement and ardent zeal.[55]

Psalm 100 ("Old Hundredth") is the best known English metrical psalms. The words are ascribed to William Kethe:

> All people that on earth do dwell,
> Sing to the Lord with cheerful voice;
> Him serve with fear His praise forth tell.
> Come ye before Him and rejoice.
>
> Know that the Lord is God indeed;
> Without our aid He did us make;
> We are His folk, He doth us feed,
> And for His sheep He doth us take.

These lines remind us that the singing of Scripture was one of the most powerful spiritual weapons for scattered congregations in the sixteenth century.

CONTROVERSY

The alleged clarity of Scripture did not, however, prevent controversy. Zwingli and Bullinger argued with Anabaptists over the Old Testament; Luther and Zwingli never did agree on the meaning of John 6; and Calvin and Servetus held different views of Christ based on different readings of the New Testament. But Scripture was clear enough to the Zurichers and Genevans that they executed dissenters.

Zurich and Anabaptists

The events of 1525 brought the issues of baptism and covenant to the fore; in the public disputations of 17 January 1525, Zwingli countered Anabaptist interpretations of Acts 19:1-10 and Matthew 28. Conrad Grebel, a member of Zwingli's circle who studied the Greek and Hebrew texts, appealed to Scripture as a dynamic force to convert

---

55. W. Stanford Reid, "The Battle Hymns of the Lord: Calvinist Psalmody of the Sixteenth Century," *Sixteenth Century Essays and Studies II,* ed. Carl S. Meyer (1971), p. 39.

sinners and destroy opponents.[56] Although Anabaptists were neither
biblicists nor fundamentalists in their use of Scripture, in 1538 the
Reformed clergy at Berne accused them of setting the New Testament
in opposition to the Old. The civil engineer and Anabaptist from Strasbourg, Pilgram Marpeck, outlined two hermeneutical problems as significant in this debate: the letter-Spirit problem in II Corinthians 3:6; and
the relation between the Old and New covenants. Infant baptism, said
Marpeck, could not be considered the New Testament equivalent of Old
Testament circumcision.[57] Marpeck accused Bucer and the Strasbourg
preachers of preaching gospel before law.[58]

Heinrich Bullinger exchanged letters with the Bernese Reformer
Berthold Haller prior to the famous 1532 Zofingen disputation. One
letter, titled *How To Act And To Dispute With Catabaptists,* states that
"half the job in dealing with Anabaptists is to be orderly. . . . What
counts is to define at the very beginning with what weapons the battle
is to be waged."[59] Bullinger's first proposition was that tension and
conflict "should be decided and clarified with Holy Scripture of Old
and New Testament." In this way he could detect "if anywhere there
lurks a negation of the Old Testament"[60] among the Anabaptists.
Bullinger also asserted that Scripture should be interpreted with the
rule of faith and love. Sermon six of the third *Decades* outlines this
view of covenant—the new covenant in Christ is nothing other than
fulfillment of the covenant with Abraham.[61]

In sum, Bullinger argued that Scripture interprets Scripture. The
choice is between the literal and the non-literal; the basis for all interpretation is faith and love. In the latter rule we see the significance of

56. William Klassen, "Anabaptist Hermeneutics: The Letter and The Spirit,"
Mennonite Quarterly Review 40 (1966):91.

57. William Klassen, "The Bern Debate of 1538," *Mennonite Quarterly Review*
40 (1966):150.

58. William Klassen, *Covenant and Community* (Grand Rapids: Eerdmans, 1968),
p. 114.

59. Heinrich Bullinger, "How to deal with Anabaptists; an unpublished letter,"
Mennonite Quarterly Review 33 (1959):84.

60. Ibid.

61. Joachim Staedke, *Die Theologie des jungen Bullinger* (Zurich: Zwingli Verlag,
1962), p. 69.

the controversy. Bullinger saw faith as the entire message of Scripture symbolized in the Apostles' Creed, and love as the servant of social order. This assumption that faith and love are the final authorities in biblical interpretation (as stated in Bullinger's letter to Haller) reveals a vital issue in Reformation hermeneutics.

Geneva and Toleration

Calvin also engaged in controversy, from his early treatise against the radicals on soul sleep to the final French version of the *Institutes*. The *Institutes* in their five Latin and four French editions expanded to take these issues into account. We will focus on two of these disputes.

Calvin attacked Servetus by name in the I John commentary of 1546-1551: In the comment on chapter one Calvin refers to the "frivolous and impudent wickedness" of Servetus. (Calvin's wrath may have been directed at Servetus' 1531 *On The Errors of the Trinity* or his 1532 *Dialogue On The Trinity*.) Servetus was a Spanish physician who worked at Basel. When he appeared in Vienna, Catholic authorities sought to burn him as a heretic. He showed up in an audience at Geneva that was listening to Calvin preach. Servetus was recognized, interrogated, and burned for trinitarian heresy in 1553.

We ask, "How could Calvin burn Servetus in Geneva with the plaudits of scholars all around?" However, as Roland Bainton reminds us: "We who are agast at the burning of one man to ashes for religion do not hesitate for the preservation of our culture to reduce whole cities to cinders."[62]

The issue involved a complex exegesis based on Hebrew works; Servetus sought to reconstruct a theology of Jewish Christianity. In this he failed.[63] But his execution raised a bitter debate between Sebastian Castellio and Theodore Beza over religious toleration. The question was, Should heretics be burned for refusal to ascribe eternity to the person of Jesus Christ the Son? Beza said yes, but Castellio argued in

---

62. Roland Bainton, *Hunted Heretic: The Life and Death of Michael Servetus, 1511-1553* (Boston: Beacon Press, 1960), p. 215.

63. Jerome Friedman, "Michael Servetus: The Case for a Jewish Christianity," *Sixteenth Century Journal* 4 (1973):87–110.

1554 for religious toleration. Curione at Basel wrote an *Apology* (under the pen name Alphonsus Lyncurius) which appealed to Matthew 18:17—a heretic is to be driven from the Church and not burned. He also cited I Corinthians 5:2 where Paul says that a heretic must be warned and avoided.[64] The magisterial Reformers countered with Titus 2:10 which states that a relapsed heretic should not live.

Beza and Castellio argued over the Matthew 13 parable of the wheat and the tares. Part of the tragedy lay in opposing Old Testament passages such as Psalm 139:21 "Do I not hate them, O Lord, that hate thee?" against gentle New Testament verses like Matthew 5:44 "Love your enemies." For Castellio, the parable of the tares was a counsel of hope and not a law for discipline. But Beza rejected Augustine's and Chrysostom's interpretation that tares should be left because they might turn into wheat. Beza argued that "The Master would have replied exactly what Moses decreed against blasphemers and contentious false prophets."[65]

Castellio's support of and Beza's reaction against Servetus provoked an extensive debate over Scripture. The use of Scripture was indeed the Reformers' concern, but at this point it led them to a dubious view of faith and love. And, although we understand the terms of the debate, we too do not recognize the need to consider Castellio's interpretation of the tares. As Roland Bainton well said: "If one may venture another interpretation, perhaps the tares might be identified with overly ingenious exegetes."[66]

Three Gods or Three Wives?

The ever-so subtle Italian refugees caused Calvin no end of trouble, whether it was Gribaldi, Gentile, Stancaro, or Ochino. And, though he was outwardly orthodox, Laelius Socinus raised the spectre of ancient heresy in Calvin's Geneva with his 1555 confession. As Philip McNair asks,

---

64. John A. Tedeschi, ed., *Italian Reformation Studies In Honor of Laelius Socinus* (Florence: Felice Le Monnier, 1965), p. 205.

65. Roland Bainton, "The Parable of the Tares as the proof text for religious liberty to the end of the sixteenth century," *Church History* 1 (1932):79.

66. Ibid., p. 89.

Was the religion of Christ trinitarian and monogamous, as the Roman Catholic Church so strenuously maintained, or unitarian and polygamous, as some of them came to suspect? Where the ingredients of Christianity *Three Gods and One Wife, or One God and Three Wives?* Such was the dilemma of the radical wing of the Italian Reformation. . . . "[67]

George Huntston Williams traces these trinitarian variations in his *Radical Reformation.* Crucial to that particular ideology is Faustus Socinus' 1578 *De Jesu Christo servatore,* which describes a human Jesus, who is savior merely through His knowledge of God. Faustus' use of *Servatore* ("servant") in his title rather than *Salvatore* ("savior") is significant. Faustus sought to focus the Christian's attention "not on an act of faith but on the conduct of life."

Delio Cantimori traces this departure from Calvin and Luther to the works of Laelius Socinus, Faustus' uncle. Laelius translated λόγος in John 1:1 as *sermo* ("talk," "conversation," "language"), and so with Erasmus viewed the Word as "pure man." The *Brevis explicatio in primum caput Evangelii Ioannis* (1590-91) pictures Christ in his poverty and humility as purely human.[68] Laelius' exegesis of John 1 led Faustus Socinus to deny on philological grounds the deity of Christ as taught by Calvin.

Bernadino Ochino of Siena fled Italy in 1542 at the age of 56. Calvin harbored Italy's most famous preacher for three years in Geneva. At first Ochino endorsed Geneva's doctrine, but Calvin mistrusted him and urged that Ochino's sermons be left in their original Italian. But when Ochino went to England in 1547, Ann Cooke translated his sermons into English.

Ochino returned to Geneva on the day after Michael Servetus was executed, and expressed his anger and sadness to Calvin. Zurich then invited Ochino to pastor its Italian congregation. When a controversy arose there over predestination, Ochino set forth four dilemmas in the

---

67. Philip McNair, "Ochino's Apology: Three Gods or Three Wives?" *History* 60 (1975):354. See also Antonio Rotondò, *Calvin and the Italian Antitrinitarians,* trans. John and Anne Tedeschi, *Reformation Essays and Studies* 2 (St. Louis: Foundation for Reformation Research, 1968).

68. Delio Cantimori, *Eretici Italiani Del Cinquecento* (Florence: G. S. Sansoni, 1939), p. 245.

Labyrinth which raised the moral issues involved in a denial of free will. Then came a volume of sermons at Basel which caused a great scandal, the *Thirty Dialogues*. *Dialogue* XXI was the crucial one, for it seemed to support polygamy. When Ochino was pressed to prove that a man cannot have more than one wife at a time, he could not do so from Scripture. The whole tone of *Dialogue* XXI is ambiguous:

> I have a wife, who so little suits with my fancy that I cannot by any means relish her; and, so far as I can hitherto perceive, she is not only barren, but unhealthy. Now, such is my disposition, that I canot be without a woman's company; and am also desirous of having children, as well for posteritysake, as for the pleasure I should take in educating my offspring in the fear of God. I might, indeed, keep a concubine or two: but that my conscience will not suffer me to do. Nay, I might wrongfully charge my wife with adultery; and so get rid of her: but in doing that, I should not only grievously offend the Almighty, but blemish my own and the poor woman's reputation, neither of which can I prevail with myself to offer at. One might likewise make her away by some dose: but of that I abhor even the very mention. Yet a thought is come into my head, which may make me easy; and that is, in plain terms, to marry another wife, without parting from her I have already: and this, according to my conception, God himself has put into my mind, and that, by Him, I am thereunto called. My desire, therefore, is, that you will resolve me, whether according to his Word, I may not lawfully do it.[69]

Such moral and exegetical subtleties were not appreciated in Zurich. Evidently, Scripture did not seem all that clear to Socini or Ochino. The logical consequence of appeal to Scripture alone led many a Scripture scholar into difficulty.

In the beginning of this chapter we quoted from Zwingli's 1522 treatise *On The Certainty and Clarity of the Word of God;*[70] we end with a particular view of Matthew 13 which shows the law of love to be at times an instrument of social coercion. It was beyond the power of exegetes to fully comprehend the mysteries of revelation in sacred Scripture. In the words of the Puritan John Robinson, "God has yet more light to break forth from his holy word."

---

69. McNair, "Ochino's Apology: Three Gods Or Three Wives?" pp. 363–64.
70. See p. 68. See p. 68.

4 | Pauline Renaissance and Catholic Crisis

Pauline theology fascinated Catholic audiences in the sixteenth century. John Colet gave lectures on the Pauline Epistles at Oxford during the 1490s; Gasparo Contarini in Venice had a conversion to "faith alone" which he described in 1511-12; Jacque LeFèvre D'Étaples in France wrote comments on the four Gospels in 1522 and in 1523 translated the New Testament into French. The work of Erasmus which led to the 1516 Greek-Latin New Testament with paraphrase and commentary is well known. All over Italy St. Paul fascinated clergy and laity. It is appropriate to apply the term *Pauline renaissance* (the title of a recent study about Puritan use of Paul) to Catholic renewal. From Colet to Contarini, Catholic scholars wrestled with the texts of Paul until Inquisition and Index redirected their search for salvation.

COMMENTARY

John Colet (c. 1467-1519)

John Colet studied at Cambridge and lectured on Paul during the 1490s at Oxford. These lectures were remarkable for their day, because, although he had other qualifications, Colet lacked a theological doctorate. Erasmus later claimed that Colet "could hardly attend to anything else but the destruction of that idol of ignorance, the cob-web divinity of the schools, and to exalt the Scriptures and Jesus Christ."[1] In a 1499 letter to Erasmus, Colet asserted that only one sense of Scripture was possible in a single passage, and that was the simplest. This letter appeared in the preface to Martin Bucer's commentary on the Gospels. It had a wide circulation in sixteenth-century Europe.[2]

One can see in these Oxford lectures a fresh approach—two decades before Luther did the same at Wittenberg.[3] This was the start of what Hubert Jedin describes in his masterly *History of the Council of Trent:*

> All over Europe during the fifteen-thirties theologians and laymen threw themselves into the study of Holy Writ: and the Fathers—especially St. Paul and St. Augustine—and experienced in themselves the meaning of sin and grace—redemption in Christ and justification by faith in Him. Their hearts' desire was to hear the words: 'I am thy salvation': passionately they wrestled with the greatest problem of the age.[4]

Colet's lectures on I Corinthians compared Scripture to Scripture. At I Corinthians 1:6 Colet marshalled references to Colossians 2:9, I John 2:20, I John 2:27, I Corinthians 1:5, John 1:14, Psalm 65:7, Ephesians 4:13 and 5:11-13, using all these passages to interpret his text. At I Corinthians 7:7 Colet illustrated the new method when he explained the person and position of Christ with fifty-two New Testament and six Old Testament references. Twenty-five of these references are from Paul.[5] The lectures conclude with the following pious thought:

> I know not whether to laugh with Democritus, or weep with Hereclitus, at the vain and profitless pursuits of men in this world; ever following with the utmost eagerness what is trivial, perishable and ephemeral; unconscious that they are being drawn to everlasting death. . . .[6]

---

1. Ernest William Hunt, *Dean Colet and His Theology* (London: S.P.C.K., 1956), p. 10.

2. Constantine Hopf, *Martin Bucer and the English Reformation* (Oxford: Basil Blackwell, 1946), p. 52.

3. Eugene F. Rice, Jr., "John Colet and the Annihilation of the Natural," *Harvard Theological Review* 45 (1952):154.

4. Hubert Jedin, *A History of the Council of Trent,* vol. 2, *The first Sessions at Trent 1545-1547* (Edinburg: Thomas Nelson and Sons, 1961) 2:168.

5. J.H. Lupton, *Ioannis Coleti Enarratio In Primam Epistolam S. Pauli Ad Corinthias* (London: George Bell and Sons, 1874), pp. 199–209. See also Hunt, *Dean Colet and His Theology*, pp. 88–102.

6. Lupton, *Ioannis Coleti Enarratio*, p. 248.

The Romans lectures touch on the Pauline themes of faith and grace. (Colet did not himself use Greek, though his contemporary at Cambridge, Richard Brinkley, knew both Greek and Hebrew.[7]) The Augustinian strain in Colet's thought—which emphasized man's radical sin—is more significant than Colet's list of fifty-eight references to I Corinthians 7:7. It led Colet to say at Romans 5:1: "Wherefore Paul concludes that justification is of faith and confidence in God alone, reconciliation to God through Jesus and restitution to grace."[8] In the comment on Romans 8:28 Colet confided to his audience that one's faith must be unflinching: Standing fast in God and Christ is a characteristic of the sons of God, who with fervent love and steadfast hope await the revelation of Christ.

Colet defined faith to his Oxford audience when he discussed Romans 9:22:

> This doctrine ... was set forth by God, through his Son, and exhibited to the world. It is the doctrine of Faith: that men should believe and trust in God, and in his messenger Jesus Christ, and confess their faith by words ... For he who has believed in Christ, and in accordance with that faith hath practiced what Christ delivered, will undoubtedly be saved.[9]

If this is not quite the Protestant 'only faith,' neither is it the scholastic 'faith formed by love.'

These lectures—which Colet continued as Dean of St. Paul's School, London—impressed many people. A letter from Colet (describing a student who came to Colet's quarters hungry for more food from Scripture) underlines Hubert Jedin's comment on the Pauline renaissance in the sixteenth century:

> I had with me yesterday evening, reverend Father, a fellow priest, a good and learned man, both an attentive listener to my expositions of St. Paul, and most anxious to gain a nearer acquaintance with the Apostle himself. After chatting for a while by the fireside, he drew forth from his bosom a little book, in which were the Epistles of St. Paul, carefully copied in his own handwriting.

---

7. W. Robert Godfrey, "John Colet of Cambridge," pp. 15–16.

8. Colet, *Romans,* ed. J. H. Lupton (London: Bell and Daldy, 1873), p. 141.

9. Ibid., pp. 49–50.

At this I smiled and quoted approvingly the words of the Gospel: 'Where your treasure is, there will your heart be also.' 'There is nothing in literature,' said he in reply, 'that I more love or admire than the writings of St. Paul.' And he was polite enough to add, with a touch of flattery, that I had done most to raise that liking of his for the Apostle, by my expositions in the previous term. I looked at him and said, 'I love you, brother, if you love St. Paul: 'Then I beg you,' he cried, 'draw forth something for me now, while we are sitting at our ease; and from this hidden treasure, which you say is so great, bring out some propositions to the light. In this way I may both have something to commit to memory, as a result of our sitting talking together, and may also be able, when reading St. Paul by myself, to catch from you some method of marking and noting down what most deserves to be noted down.' 'I will oblige you, my good sir,' I said, 'Open your book, and let us try how many golden sentences can be gathered in the first chapter of Romans alone.' And so, reverend Father, I have felt a wish to copy out for you what he wrote at my dictation; that you too, ardent lover as you are of all holier wisdom, may see what points we lightly touched upon in our beloved St. Paul, while sitting the other day by our winter fireside, though we went no farther than the first chapter of Romans. These are as follows: Faith in Christ comes of calling by grace. Preaching Christ comes from separation. Paul was commissioned and sent by Christ Himself. All true Christians are beloved of God and holy. Grace and peace with God are what is most to be sought for from God. The chief source of joy and congratulation is the faith of men. Others are to be visited for the fruit and profit of faith. It is the duty of a preacher of the word of God to teach all alike. . . .[10]

Gasparo Contarini (1483-1542)

In 1542 Cardinal Gasparo Contarini died,[11] worn out in part from the failure to reconcile the Protestant and Catholic viewpoints at the Ratisbon Colloquy of 1541. In May of that year Protestant and Cath-

---

10. J. H. Lupton, *A Life of John Colet D.D.* (London: George Bell and Sons, 1909), pp. 90–92.

11. James Bruce Ross, "The Emergence of Gasparo Contarini: A Bibliographical Essay," *Church History* 41 (1972):22–45.

olic representatives did agree on justification by faith, but failure to agree on the Eucharist prevented any permanent accord.[12] (Contarini manipulated the agenda so that papal authority was not the first item to be discussed.)

In 1537 Contarini, the Venetian Cardinal, nobleman, and scholar, had chaired the Reform Commission which reported to Pope Paul III on abuses in the church. Contarini himself presented the report to Pope Paul III, which reads in part:

> The origin of these evils was due to the fact that some popes, your predecessors, in the words of the Apostle Paul, 'having itching ears heaped up to themselves teachers according to their own lusts.' . . . From this source as from a Trojan horse so many abuses and such grave diseases have rushed in upon the Church of God that we now see her afflicted almost to the despair of salvation. . . .[13]

Contarini was converted to the idea of salvation by faith alone in 1512, which he described in biblical commentaries thirty years later. Contarini was the most impressive thinker in the circle of Italian Reformers who shared Luther's view of faith.[14]

In 1959 Hubert Jedin published thirty letters of Contarini written between the years 1511-1523. Using the letters to document a Catholic religious experience parallel and prior to Luther's,[15] Jedin claims that Contarini intended to become a monk. Though Contarini entered Venetian civic life rather than a monastery, his religious experience was real

12. See Peter Matheson, *Cardinal Contarini at Regensburg* (Oxford: Clarendon Press, 1972), pp. 114–21 for a discussion of the use of Scripture. Also see Basil Hall's excellent survey of these attempts in his article, "The Colloquies between Catholics and Protestants, 1539-41" ed. G.J. Cuming and Derek Baker, *Councils and Assemblies* (Cambridge: At The University Press, 1971), pp. 235–66.

13. John C. Olin, *The Catholic Reformation* (New York: Harper & Row, 1969), pp. 186–87.

14. Elizabeth Gleason, "Cardinal Gasparo Contarini (1483-1542) and the Beginning of Catholic Reform" (Ph.D. diss, Stanford University, 1963). This thesis is the best study of the mature Contarini.

15. Hubert Jedin, "Contarini und Camaldoi," *Archivio Italiano per la Storia della Pieta* 2 (1952):53–117.

enough, as one letter in particular states.[16] Its date is Easter 1511, when Contarini questioned the reality of penance. He concluded:

> We must attempt merely to unite ourselves with this, our head, with faith, with hope, and with such little love as we are capable of. . . . He was quick to accept me and to cause His Father to cancel the debt I had contracted which I by myself was incapable of satisfying.[17]

The last of these thirty letters is dated 7 February 1523:

> No one can justify himself by his works or purge himself from his inclinations. One must turn to the divine grace which can be obtained through faith in Jesus Christ as St. Paul said: . . . Whence I conclude that every living man is a thing of vanity and that one must justify oneself through another's righteousness, i.e. through Christ's and when one joins oneself to Him His righteousness becomes ours, nor must we then depend upon ourselves even in the slightest degree.[18]

These sentiments are not unique ones, for the Venetian laity in particular shared much of the nobleman's concern.[19] And the similarity to Luther is remarkable.[20] (We know that the Lutheran *Opera* were on sale in Venice, since Sanudo the Diarist tells us he owned a copy in 1521.)[21]

Contarini consistently held to papal primacy, which kept him firmly Catholic. This view can be seen in his first theological work: *A Confutation of Lutheran Articles or Questions.* Contarini summarized the *Augs-*

---

16. Felix Gilbert, "Religion and Politics in the Thought of Gasparo Contarini," ed. Theodore Rabb and Jerrold Seigel, *Action and Conviction In Early Modern Europe* (Princeton University Press, 1969), p. 94.

17. Heinz Mackensen, "Contarini's Theological Role at Ratisbon in 1541," *Archiv für Reformationsgeschichte* 51 (1960):52–53.

18. Ibid., p. 55.

19. O.M.T. Logan, "Grace and Justification: Some Italian Views of the Sixteenth and Early Seventeenth Centuries," *Journal of Ecclesiastical History* 20 (1969):67–78. See also Anne Jacobson Schutte, "The *Lettere Volgari* and the Crisis of Evangelism in Italy," *Renaissance Quarterly* 28 (1975):639–88.

20. See J.B. Ross, "Gasparo Contarini and His Friends," *Studies In The Renaissance* 17 (1970):204–32.

21. Ross, "The Emergence of Gasparo Contarini," p. 44 n.163.

burg Confession in his refutation. (His brother-in-law had been Orator at the Augusburg Diet, and through him Contarini obtained an eye-witness account.)[22] In this work Contarini did not yet accept the altered Lutheran view of faith which appears in the 1541 Ratisbon context.[23] Between 1530 and 1541 stands the Reform report of 1537 and more complete access to the works of Luther, Melanchthon, Bucer, and Calvin.

Contarini's last works were a series of commentaries on the Pauline epistles. As early as 26 December Contarini wrote of his desire to study Scripture[24] and a treatise of 1541 instructed preachers to cease squabbling about finer points of doctrine.[25] In 1542 came the mature reflections on Paul's epistles. From 1511 to 1541 the Venetian Reformer saw that faith alone had the power to save. Contarini's commentaries of 1542 reflect this insight on faith which he shared with Luther and Calvin.

The biblical *scholia* on almost every page reaffirm Contarini's thirty-year resolve to trust for salvation in Christ, who alone is the power and wisdom of God. Twenty-five years earlier Contarini had indicated concern about Savonarola, the Florentine preacher-prophet burned in 1498 for his use of Scripture.[26] Now on Romans 1:17 Contarini comments:

(From faith to faith) . . . actually, *from faith,* refers to God who promised and gave faith to us. *To faith,* truly refers to us, whose assent and confidence rest in the divine promises and faith, which is given to us by God.[27]

At Galatians 3 Contarini repeats this theme with urgency: "Through faith in Christ we possess the promise of the remission of sins and the inheritance of eternal life."[28]

---

22. Gleason, *Cardinal Gasparo Contarini,* p. 77.

23. Ibid., pp. 78–79.

24. Jedin, *Contarini und Camaldoli,* p. 25, l. 7–10.

25. Gleason, *Cardinal Gasparo Contarini,* pp. 198–99.

26. Felix Gilbert, "Contarini on Savonarola: An Unknown Document of 1516," *Archiv für Reformationsgeschichte* 59 (1968):149.

27. *Gasparis Contarini Cardinalis Opera* (Paris: Sebastian Nivellius, 1571), *Scholia In Epistolae Pauli,* p. 435.

28. Ibid., p. 479.

Romans 4 and 5 continue this theme, that man in God's presence needs the forgiveness of sins, and that God's promises initiate justification. Contarini argued that the Vulgate mistranslates Romans 4, where the Latin read: "And from faith and according to grace that the promise may be firm." Contarini changed the *and* to *in order that,* making faith prior to grace. According to Contarini, grace and faith are dependent on the antecedent promises of God. God justifies by grace so that one relies totally on His promise. Contarini sums up the issue in Romans 4:

> But therefore according to grace, to the end that the promise may be firm, for if the matter depended on justice so that we would be rewarded according to God's grace, the promise would have no certainty because of the lack of our good works.[29]

Page after page of these notes to Paul's epistles confirm that the Cardinal faced a crisis. It was difficult to reconcile trust in the promises of God and confidence in the papacy of his day. Contarini avoided the paradox of that position by relating papal authority primarily to discipline and only secondarily to dogma.[30] Contarini's crisis was also a result of the aristocratic sentiments which he shared with refined circles of Italians; sentiments which appealed neither to the papacy nor to large numbers of people.

The Inquisition and Index of forbidden books dampened this diverse Italian Pauline renaissance. The crisis—and a fascinating episode in Italian Reform—ended with Contarini, whose heart was in the study of the truths of Pauline teaching. He accepted them—as did Luther after him —and defended them in the year of the Italian Inquisition.

Juan de Valdés (c. 1500-1541)

From the Oxford lectures of Colet and the crisis of the Italian Cardinal Contarini, we turn briefly to the Spanish Reformer Juan de Valdés. Between 1535-1541, at his villa in a beautiful quarter of Naples, his friends gathered for Sunday morning prayer, meditation, and discus-

---

29. Ibid., pp. 437–38.

30. Gleason, *Cardinal Gasparo Contarini*, p. 204.

sion. From these meetings rose the *One Hundred and Ten Considerations,* a translation and Spanish commentary on the Psalms and commentaries on Matthew, Romans, and Corinthians. The selections in the *One Hundred and Ten Considerations* vary in length from two to nine pages.

Bernardino Ochino (discussed in chapter three) would get notes from Valdés each evening before he preached in Naples.[31] Pietro Martire Vermigli, the Italian Augustinian who fled Italy in 1542, belonged to Valdés' circle. Their kind of "evangelical catholicism" led them to search Scripture for help with problems of everyday living. Even seventeenth-century England used the *Considerations* at Little Gidding. Indeed, T.S. Eliot wrote a poem by that title: *Little Gidding.*[32]

Valdés' *Dialogue* analyzes the Lord's Prayer as found in Matthew 6 and Luke 11. "Deliver us from evil" prompted Valdés to state that God delivers one from evil in the flesh, for one "will eat of and support himself with the daily bread of God's grace and the Holy Spirit. . . ."[33]

Curione published an Italian translation of the *One Hundred and Ten Considerations* at Basel in 1550; in his preface Curione praises Valdés' work as a "great and heavenly treasure."[34] The *Considerations* had the greatest impact of any Valdesian writing. Curione's preface challenges the other theological writers of his day:

> [They have] drawn all the Scriptures to Questions and Disputations, and made as it were an Academy thereof, raising such doubts in everything. . . . With their ample and infinite volumes, they have withdrawn and estranged men from the studie of the truly holy scriptures . . . and instead of Christs disciples have made men mens scholars: so that we are come to that passe that more and greater credit is given to those which are termed Doctours . . . then to the simple doctrine of Christ himself.[35]

31. George H. Williams and Angel M. Mergal, *Spiritual and Anabaptist Writers* (Philadelphia: Westminster Press, 1957), p. 304.

32. T.S. Eliot, *Little Gidding* (London: Faber and Faber, 1942).

33. Williams and Mergal, *Spiritual and Anabaptist Writers,* p. 327.

34. Ibid., p. 331.

35. John Valdés, *Divine/Considerations/Treating/Of Those Things which are most profi/table, most necessary, and most perfect in our Christian Profession,* trans. Nicholas Ferrar (Cambridge: Printed for E.D. by Roger Daniel, Printer to the University, 1646), pp. 3^r–4^v.

In Consideration 54 Valdés claims that "prayer and consideration are two books or Interpreters very sure . . . to [explain] holy scripture."[36] "Prayer discovers the way, and opens, and manifesteth it: And Consideration puts a man into it, and makes him walk therein."[37] According to Valdés, it is God who inspires one to pray; consideration is the experience of things written in holy Scripture.

Valdés declares himself of one mind with two authorities: St. Paul and David. Valdés quotes I Corinthians 1:16 ("Even as the testimony of Jesus Christ is confirmed in you") to show that he first prays that God might open Scripture, and then considers within himself, "of what Christian matters I have any experience."[38] David's "For I am a stranger with thee" also leads Valdés to prayer first, then this consideration:

> I go examining in what manner I am a Pilgrim, and stranger in this present life. . . . And finding likewise that God in this self same manner is a Pilgrim in the world . . . I understand, that in this manner the Saints of the Law were strangers with God; and in this manner are the Saints of the Gospel, and amongst them as the head the Son of God our Lord.[39]

"I am a stranger with thee" is an appropriate theme from Hebrews 13:13-14 for the Italian exiles who published the *Considerations* in the sixteenth century. Consideration 55 goes on to explain that neither knowledge nor curiousity will interpret Scripture, but only experience and simplicity.

The Matthew commentary was published during this same period, and was circulated widely in Europe.[40] A good example of Valdés' exegesis is his comment on Matthew 3:7-10 (where John the Baptist accuses the religious leaders of Israel of repenting out of fear):

> We who have repented bear testimony to our Christian faith by living mortified as to the flesh and Quickened as to the Spirit. . . .

---

36. Ibid , p. 192.

37. Ibid., p. 193.

38. Ibid., p. 194.

39. Ibid., pp. 195–96.

40. Carolo Ossola, "Un Contributo Alla Storia Della Spiritualita Valdesiana In Italia: Tradizione E. Traduzione Del Commento A Matteo Di Juan De Valdes," *Rivista di Storia e Letteratura Religiosa* 9 (1973):62–68.

Confidence in Christian regeneration is efficient in man to make him live in holiness and righteousness all the days of his life. . . .[41]

CONFESSION

Catholic Reformation or Counter Reformation—which expression shall we use? Either term, however, hints of controversy and conflict. The irenic and charitable character of Contarini is contrasted with the stern Carafa, hammer of heretics, and who, as Pope Paul IV, was suspicious of Cardinals such as Pole and Morone (both presidents of the Council of Trent). Even Ignatius Loyola, founder of the Jesuits, came under suspicion in Spain. The Spanish Inquisition in Alcalá (1526) threatened Loyola with capital punishment. "Later, in Paris (1529), Venice (1537) and Rome (1538) he was again and again brought in for inquisitorial investigation."[42]

Ignatius Loyola (1491-1556)

Ignatius Loyola and his disciple missionary Francis Xavier were Basque. And who indeed are better shepherds than the Basque; and who were finer shepherds than Loyola to the Europeans or Xavier to Christ's sheep in Asia? Legend has it that both Jesuits were born in stables where their mothers retired in honor of Bethlehem's ministry. But James Broderick drily remarks: "Neither of them began his imitation of Christ as early as all that. . . ."[43]

Loyola, the former soldier and visionary, entered the College de Montaigu on 2 February 1528. Few have begun Latin study at age thirty-seven as Loyola did in Paris. But Loyola showed that it is pos-

41. Juan De Valdes, *Commentary on the Gospel of St. Matthew* trans. John Betts (London: Trubner & Co., 1882), pp. 34–35.

42. Robert E. McNally, "The Council of Trent and the Spiritual Doctrine of the Counter Reformation," *Church History* 34 (1965):43.

43. James Broderick, *The Origin of the Jesuits* (London: Longmans, Green and Co., 1940), p. 5.

sible for an ablative absolute to have a profound impact on the kingdom of God. In 1534 Loyola (who now had his Master of Arts degree)
and several followers vowed to reach Jerusalem in a year or place themselves under the papal sword. In 1539 Pope Paul III received the group
and in 1540 established the Jesuit Order with the bull, *Rules of the
Militant Church.* By the time Loyola died in 1556 his followers had
multiplied into a thousand whose obedience compensated Rome for the
loss of Luther.

Loyola's *Rules for Thinking with the Church* appeared as the final
section of the *Spiritual Exercises* while Loyola was in Paris (1528-35).
Rule 13 has become notorious: "If we wish to proceed securely in all
things, we must hold fast to the following principle: What seems to me
white I will believe black if the hierarchical Church so defines."[44] The
Council of Sens influenced these rules with its own condemnation of
Lutheran errors in France.[45]

More positive biblical themes permeate Loyola's *Spiritual Exercises.*
Robert McNally finds in the *Exercises* the great motifs of salvation
history, in which the Kingdom of God and Obedience alternate as
optimistic and humanistic themes.[46] The world is good, God is good,
and man is good in the Ignatian scheme of imaginative biblicism. One
example contemplates the nativity by reconstructing it mentally: "It
will consist here in seeing in the imagination the way from Nazareth to
Bethlehem; consider its length, its breadth; whether level or through
valleys and over hills."[47]

Personal reform and renewal lie at the heart of sixteenth-century
Catholic spirituality. In the Jesuit colleges biblical truth often broke
through the academic and polemical structures. That is one way the
Bible led to confession in Catholicism: by obedience.

---

44. John C. Olin, *The Catholic Reformation,* (Westminister, Md: Christian Classics, Inc., 1969), p. 210.

45. McNally, "The Council of Trent," p. 42.

46. Ibid., p. 40.

47. Ibid., p. 41.

Vittoria Colonna

1543 was a remarkable year. The Polish astronomer Copernicus published *On The Revolution of The Heavenly Bodies* and Vesalius published *On The Fabric of The Human Body*. That year also saw a religious book appear in Venice with the title *The Benefits of Jesus Christ Crucified*. In this Italian book, along with sonnets of Vittoria di Colonna, a pattern of Catholic biblicism emerges. Vittoria, a wealthy widow from the Italian nobility, was an inspiration for Michaelangelo. The artist wrote poetry for her and sculpted for her a statue of Christ. Michaelangelo wrote to the Marchese:

> Wearied and anxious in my
> troubled mind, seeking where'er
> I may salvation find:
> Like one to whom the stars
> by clouds are crossed,
> Who, turn which way he will,
> errs and is lost,
> Therefore take thou my hearts
> unwritten page,
> And write thou on it
> What is wanted there!

The Colonna family had been famous in Italy since 1050. Sciara Colonna, for example, in 1303 attacked Pope Boniface VIII with three hundred horsemen, and even struck the pope with his own gauntlet. (The poet Dante immortalized his horror at such desecration of the papal office.)

Vittoria Colonna was born in 1490 and was sent to the Neopolitan island of Ischia. Vittoria sorrowed at the death of her warrior husband who died seventeen years after she married him in 1509. At age 36 this tall, blond widow wrote sonnets of sorrow which she followed with songs of salvation. Vittoria moved in the biblical circles of Valdés at Naples and Cardinal Pole at Viterbo, and her sonnets mirror the biblical concerns of both Reformers.

Sorrow for her dead husband led Vittoria to write sonnets of deep feeling:

> Am I able in the bitter and black tempest
> of this miserable world to enter into the Ark
> with Noah, the beloved of God, when no other bark
> can be found in the perilous and dark waters?
> or can I with the Hebrew host thank God!
> singing in joy and festivity on the further shore,
> when they had boldly and quickly
> passed over the Red Sea? Or with Peter, does my heart
> feel itself supported by the Divine hand, when my faith
> fails to support me on the heaving waves?
> Ah! if I am not equal to these things,
> yet the favor of heaven
> is not removed nor lessened;
> nor is its succour slow.

On the isle of Ischia (where she stayed from 1526-28) she wrote directly of her faith in Christ. Her Sonnet 66 says:

> When the troubled sea rises and surrounds a firm rock
> with its impetuous and furious waves,
> if it stands secure, the tempestuous pride is broken,
> and the wave falls back into itself.
> So I, if against me the deep waters
> of any angry world rage,
> lift to heaven my eyes as from a rock
> and the greater their strength,
> the more does my strength abound!
> And if the storm of desire renews the combat,
> I run to the shore, and, with a cord entwined
> of love and faith, I fasten my bark
> to that on which I rely, Jesus the Living Rock;
> so that when I will, I can always enter the harbor.

Vittoria's association with Valdés, Pole, and Contarini raised her spirits
to trust in Christ alone, as she expresses in Sonnet 48:

> Ofttimes I flee to God, through ice and mists,
> for light and heat to melt my frozen nature;
> and when my soul continues cold and dark,
> at least her thoughts are ever turned to heaven,
> and in great silence she listens
> for that still, small voice,
> which only the soul can hear, which says, Fear not:
> Jesus, that wide and deep sea, is come into this world
> to give rest to all who are heavy laden.
> The waves of this eternal sea
> are ever sweet and bright
> to all who, in humble trust,
> embark upon the great deeps
> of His goodness.[48]

So we see that both Catholic women and men found comfort in Pauline
faith before their fragile association splintered in 1542, the year Contarini died. Also in 1542, Ochino (with Peter Martyr) fled the Italian
Inquisition to join the Protestant Scripture battles of Northern Europe.

The Beneficio di Cristo

The finest summary of Pauline faith in Italy was Benedeto of Man-
tua's *Trattato utilissimo del beneficio di Giesu Christo crocifisso, verso i
Christiani* (referred to above as *The Benefits of Jesus Christ Crucified*).
All copies were thought to have been destroyed, but in 1855 Charles
Babington located a copy in St. John's College Library, Cambridge. It
has consistently provoked intense debate—from the sixteenth-century
Catholic Ambrosio Catharinus to Tommaso Bozza in the twentieth cen-
tury. Catharinus rejected it as Lutheran, and Bozza claims that whole

---

48. Mrs. Henry Roscoe, *Vittoria Colonna: Her Life and Poems* (London: Mac-
Millan and Co., 1863), p. 330. See also Alan Bullock, "Three New Poems by
Vittoria Colonna," *Italian Studies* 24 (1969):44–54. Also Roland Bainton,
"Vittoria Colonna," in *Women of the Reformation In Germany and Italy* (Minne-
apolis: Augsburg, 1971), pp. 201–18. See the study "Vittoria Colonna poétesse"
in Suzanne Therault, *Un Cénacle Humaniste de la Renaissance Autour di Vittoria
Colonna Châtelaine d'Ischia* (Paris: Marcel Didier, 1968), pp. 133–99.

sections of Calvin's 1539 *Institutes* occur in the text.[49] But whatever scholars conclude about its composition, the beauty of this document bears witness to the absorption of Pauline spirituality in Italian Catholic circles. The title seems a double allusion to Melanchthon's phrase in the 1521 *Loci Communes:* "To know Jesus Christ is to know his benefits," and to Thomas à Kempis' fifteenth-century tract, which included this phrase in the title.

For his criticism, Catharinus relied on a 1542 copy of the *Beneficio,* and the excerpts he used in his attack vary from the 1543 Venetian printed edition. Chapter six had been altered to teach confidence in the "most holy predestination" which "maintains the true Christian in a state of continual, spiritual joy."[50]

In 1538-39 Contarini had supported a similar view. Also, Philip Melanchthon's 1521 *Loci Communes* had distinguished between (and harmonized) forensic justification and the infusion of grace by the Spirit. The *Beneficio* did the same. In fact, the sacramental discussion in chapter five of the *Beneficio* paraphrases Calvin's 1539 *Institutes.* Especially arresting is the following selection which parallels the 1536 *Institutes* and echoes Luther's 1520 *Freedom of a Christian Man.* Small wonder the Inquisition sought to remove the *Beneficio* from the reach of Catholic readers! Compare the following section from the *Beneficio*:

> Christ took on our poverty, in order to give us his riches; he took on our infirmity, to confirm us with his strength; he became mortal, to make us immortal; he descended to the earth so we could ascend to heaven; and he became the Son of Man together with us in order to make us sons of God with him.[51]

with a parallel selection from Calvin's *Institutes* (1539):

> This is the wonderful exchange which, out of his measureless benevolence, he has made with us; that, becoming Son of man with us, he has made us sons of God with him; that, by his

---

49. Valdo Vinay, "Die Schrift Il Beneficio di Christo und ihre Verbreitung in Euopa nach der neueren Forschurg," *Archiv für Reformationgeschichte* 58 (1967):29–72. See also Tommaso Bozza, *Il Beneficio Di Cristo,* Nuovi Studi Sulla Riforma In Italia, I (Rome: Edizioni Di Storia E Letteratura, 1976).

50. Ruth Prelowski, "The Beneficio Di Cristo translated, with an Introduction," ed. John Tedeschi, *Italian Reformation Studies,* p. 85.

51. Ibid., p. 81.

descent to earth, he has prepared an ascent to heaven for us; that, by taking on our mortality, he has conferred his immortality upon us; that, accepting our weakness, he has strengthened us by his power; that, receiving our poverty unto himself, he has transferred his wealth to us; that, taking the weight of our iniquity upon himself (which oppressed us), he has clothed us with his righteousness.

The *Beneficio* insists on justification by faith alone, allows no merit for subsequent works, gives Holy Scripture the highest authority, and supports its arguments from Paul and the patristic fathers.[52] The treatise quotes from Paul's Epistle to the Philippians and parallels the concerns of Luther and Calvin:

I do not have my own justice, which consists in the works of the Law, but the justice that consists in the faith of Christ, which is a gift of God, that is, the justice of faith, which allows me to come to a knowledge of him.
Oh, these are most significant words that every Christian ought to engrave on his heart, and ask God to make him fully appreciate them! Here you see how clearly St. Paul shows that whoever truly knows Christ considers the works of the Law harmful, to the extent that they lead man away from trust in Christ, on whom he should base his whole salvation, and they make him rely on himself. Then extending this judgement [sentenza], St. Paul adds that he holds everything dung in order to gain Christ and to be incorporated into him, pointing out that whoever trusts in works and claims to justify himself with them, does not gain Christ and become incorporated in Him. Since the whole mystery of faith consists of this truth, and St. Paul wanted to make his meaning better understood, he adds and impresses upon them that he rejects every exterior justification, every justice founded upon the observance of the Law, and that he embraces the justice given by God through faith. God gives justice to those who believe that in Christ he has chastised all our sins, and that Christ, as St. Paul himself says, 'has made himself our wisdom, justice, sanctification and redemption, so that, as it is written, let him who glories, glory in the Lord, and not in his own words. . . . Most beloved brethren, let us not follow the stupid opinion of the foolish Galatians but the truth that St. Paul teaches, and let us give all the glory of our justification to the mercy of God and to the merits of his Son, who with his blood has released us from the dominion

---

52. Ibid., p. 31.

of the Law and the tyranny of sin and death, and has led us to
the kingdom of God to give us eternal happiness. I say he has
freed us from the command of the Law, because he has given us
his Spirit, that teaches us every truth, and he has perfectly satis-
fied the Law. He has given this satisfaction to all his members,
that is, to all true Christians, so that they can appear confidently
before the tribunal of God, because they are clothed in the justice
of his Christ and because he has freed them from the curses of the
Law. Thus the Law can no longer accuse or condemn us; it can no
longer arouse our affections and appetites or increase our sin, and
for this reason St. Paul says that the chirograph, which was un-
favorable to us, has been cancelled by Christ and annulled on the
wood of the cross. Because our Christ freed us from the dominion
of the Law, he has also released us from the tyranny of sin and of
death, which can no longer oppress us because they have been
overcome by Christ (and consequently by we who are his members) through his resurrection. Thus we can say with St. Paul and
with the prophet Hosea: "Death has been conquered and destroyed. Death, where is your sting? Hell, where is your victory?
The sting of death is sin, and the power of sin is the law, but let
us thank God who has granted us victory through Jesus Christ our
Lord." He is that most happy seed, who has crushed the head of
the poisonous serpent, namely the devil, so that all who believe
in Christ and place their whole trust in his grace, will conquer sin,
death, the devil, and hell, with him. He is that blessed seed of
Abraham, in whom God promised to bless all nations. Previously
everyone had to fight that horrible serpent on his own and free
himself from the curse, but this enterprise was so difficult, that
all the forces of the world put together could not accomplish it.
Then our God, the father of mercy, was moved to pity by our
miseries, and gave us his only-begotten Son who has freed us from
the serpent's poison, and who has been made our blessing and
justification, provided that we completely renounce all our exterior justification in accepting him. Most beloved brethren, let us
embrace the justice of our Jesus Christ, making it our own by
means of faith; let us firmly hold that we are just, not through
our works but through the merits of Christ; and let us live, happy
and confident that the justice of Christ annihilates all our injus-
tice, and makes us good, just and holy in the sight of God. For
when God sees us incorporated into his Son through faith, he will
no longer think of us as children of Adam, but as his own children, and he will make us, together with his legitimate Son, heirs
of all his riches.[53]

---

53. Ibid., pp. 54–55.

This treatise, with obvious accents from Luther and Calvin, is the finest document to come from the abortive Italian Reformation. A recent study, however, suggests that distinctive Protestant accents were added to the 1542 manuscript before its 1543 Venetian printing.[54]

CONTROVERSY

Reginald Pole (1500-1558)

Catholic response to Luther culminated in the Council of Trent. Cardinal Pole, member of the Reform commission of 1536-37, opened the sessions with a sermon based on the prophet Ezekiel.

Pole indicted the Council fathers on three counts. He claimed that they fostered heresy, furthered a decline in morality, and supported war. Ezekiel 20:1-4 together with references to Ezra, Nehemiah, and Daniel supported Pole's warning at Trent that the theologians must permit humanistic and evangelical interpretations of Paul.[55] Controversy over these issues focused in Trent's 1546-47 debates on Scripture and on justification.[56] Pole urged the Council participants to shoulder their burden:

> Before the tribunal of God's mercy we, the shepherds should make ourselves responsible for all the evils now burdening the flock of Christ. The sins of all we should take upon ourselves . . . because the truth is that of these evils we are in great part the cause, and therefore we should implore the divine mercy through Jesus Christ.[57]

Reginald Pole was favored by King Henry VIII, and in 1519 the King sent his royal humanist kinsman to Italy. Pole studied at Padua and

---

54. Carlo Ginzburg and Adriano Prosperi, "Le Due Redazioni Del Beneficio Di Cristo," in *Eresia e Riforma Nell' Italia del Cinquecento,* ed. Albano Biondi et al (Chicago: The Newberry Library, 1974), pp. 137–204. Tommaso Bozza's latest analysis rejects this line of inquiry. He suggests that it rests upon brave words, gross errors, false interpretations, and absurd conclusions that reveal ignorance of the theology of Reform. See Bozza, *Il Beneficio Di Cristo,* p. 389.

55. Delio Cantimori, "Italy and the Papacy," *The New Cambridge Modern History,* vol. 2, *The Reformation* 1520-59, p. 270.

56. See my "Trent and Justification (1546): A Protestant Reflection," *Scottish Journal of Theology* 21 (1968):385–406.

57. Ibid., p. 385.

joined a biblical study circle in the Benedictine monastery at Venice.
There Cortese, Contarini, and Pole—all eventual members of the Papal
Reform Commission—studied the Gospels and Pauline epistles.

In the four years before the Reform Commission met in 1536, Pole
gave special attention to biblical study, which included the Old Testament. During 1534 in particular Pole's correspondence was laced with
biblical references.

While in Liége on a diplomatic mission (1537) Pole lectured on Paul.
As one of his students describes:

> Every other day, the legate [Pole] lectures to us on the epistles of
> St. Paul, beginning with the first epistle to Timothy. . . . How
> often has the legate said to me: 'Surely this peace is given to us
> by God!'[58]

The year 1541 saw Cardinal Pole in Viterbo with several followers of
Valdés. Vittoria Colonna was present, and so was the poet Flaminio.
Pole served as a papal governor and spiritual advisor to the transplanted
Valdesian circle at Viterbo where Benedeto of Mantua, author of the
Beneficio di Cristo was a member in 1542. The circle was crowded with
poets, aristocratic ladies, cardinals, and the future Protestants Peter
Martyr Vermigli and Ochino, all reading Paul. They also read patristic
literature and Protestant works such as Calvin's 1539 *Institutes.*[59]

1542 marks the internal disintegration of this Italian Catholic spiritual party. In spite of his committement to the *Beneficio di Cristo* which
shared the Protestant reliance on Scripture, faith alone, and predestination, Cardinal Pole was reluctant to commit himself publically. His
advice to Vittoria Colonna has been widely quoted: "to believe as
if . . . salvation depended upon faith alone, and to act, on the other
hand, as if it depended upon good works."[60]

The Cardinal scholar of Henry VIII, confidant of the Valdesian 'spir-
ituali' and reforming Cardinals, fought his own crisis at Trent. There as

58. Angelo Maria Quirini, *Epistolarum Reginaldi Poli S.R.E. Cardinalis et aliorum
ad ipsum II* (Brecia: Joannes-Maria Rizzardi, 1746), p. 104–105.

59. See Dermot Fenlon, *Heresy and Obedience in Tridentine Italy: Cardinal Pole
and the Counter-Reformation* (Cambridge: At the University Press, 1972),
pp. 69–88.

60. Ibid., p. 96.

president of the Council, Pole defended *sola fide* in the debates about justification until he retired with a diplomatic illness. But first came the battle over Scripture at Trent, in which Pole was not alone.[61]

The two presidents of the Council, Pole and Cervini, wished to discuss the decree of the Council of Florence (4 February 1441). But Del Monte declared on 12 February that by formal Canon Law the decree must stand, and so the canonicity of Scripture and varying degrees of authority within it were not then open to debate.[62] After many proposals and meetings within the three sections headed by the legates, Giacomo Nachianti, Bishop of Chioggia, astonished the general congregation.[63] On 26 February 1546 Nachianti warned the Council that tradition was not equal to Scripture; Trent then took up the question of biblical reform. Girolamo Seripando supported the doctrine of the purity of Scripture in the debate on 1 March. As Hubert Jedin relates:

> Seripando moreover demanded that preachers should be prepared for their work by a better training in biblical exegesis. When he spoke thus, Seripando countered without naming him, the attack made by the Bishop of Bertinoro, who had spoken before him, on the philological and literal interpretation of Holy Scripture.[64]

The 22 March draft of the decree created much criticism over the formula, 'partly ... partly.' The General of the Servites, Conuccio, rejected this formula, claiming that the stream of revelation could not be divided into Scripture and tradition. Conuccio said that Scripture was complete and contained all truths necessary to salvation. When the Bishop of Feltre argued over the parity of Scripture and tradition, Cervini silenced them both.[65]

> There can be no doubt that though the majority of the theologians of Trent may not have approved the formula partim ... partim, they approved the thing itself, that is, the statement that dogmatic tradition was a channel of revelation which supplemented the Scriptures.[66]

---

61. Ibid., pp. 116–36.

62. Ibid., p. 55.

63. Ibid., p. 64. Jedin also calls this appeal to Scripture a Lutheran warning.

64. Ibid., p. 69.

65. Ibid., pp. 74–75.

66. Ibid., p. 75.

Linked with this discussion was the issue of revision of the Vulgate upon which rested to a great extent the dogmatic tradition of the Latin Church.[67] The general congregation of 1 April again faced the question of tradition and Scripture. Rather than "equality" or "parity" between tradition and Scripture, the new phrase suggested was "similar piety and affection."[68] The formulation was important, for it represented the view of the new biblical theology which included Pole and Seripando.[69] Hubert Jedin tells us that:

> Seripando belonged to the minority, which stood for the clause 'similis pietate affectus' in place of the 'par pietatis affectus' (dub 7) and so wished to prevent making traditions equal to Holy Scripture. To this minority belonged the ablest and most active fathers of the Council; who in the use of Holy Scripture had taken a common stand with respect to the draft of the decree.[70]

Del Monte refused to permit debate on matters not included in the day's programme, unless proposed by a legate. This forstalled a counterattack by Pacheco, who held that reading of the Bible by the laity was the source of all heresies. But on 3 April his demand was renewed in the following terms: "All translations other than the Vulgate, even the Septuagint, must be forbidden."[71] It was never the Council's intention to find the whole of doctrine in Scripture *and* the whole in tradition. When one turns to the historical evidence of the bitter opposition at Trent, such a synthesis is impossible to maintain.

The problem of the parity of Scripture and tradition was not solved on 5 April 1546. The Cardinal of Trent disagreed whether lay people should be permitted to produce commentaries on the Bible. The Cardi-

---

67. F. J. Crehan, S.J., "The Bible in the Roman Catholic Church from Trent to the Present Day," in *The Cambridge History of the Bible,* ed. S.L. Greenslade, vol. 3, *The West from the Reformation to the Present Day,* 3:204.

68. Hubert Jedin, *Papal Legate at the Council of Trent: Cardinal Seripando,* (St. Louis: Herder, 1947), p. 279.

69. See Ibid., p. 290 for a description of Pole's toleration of vernacular translations.

70. Ibid., p. 279.

71. Jedin, *A History of the Council of Trent,* II, pp. 83–84. See also Robert McNally, "The Council of Trent and Vernacular Bibles," *Theological Studies* 27 (1966):213–18.

nal appealed to Pole as arbiter, but Pole declined to decide the issue.[72] On 5 April Nachianti created a furor by attacking the equality of tradition with Scripture. He labeled such dual views of revelation impious, and his outburst had the support of Seripando.[73]

At a conference with the committee members in the course of the afternoon of 5th April, to which the Dominican Ambrosius Catharinus was likewise invited, the legates yielded to the minority and replaced the 'equally' of the decree by 'similarly' even though the vote of 1st April had settled the question. In the particular congregations which were convened for 6th April, the whole subject was examined once more, with the result that the alteration had to be changed back again. For Bonuccio even the term 'similarly' went too far. Only in the general congregation of 7th April was the decree finally approved. At this very latest moment partim-partim was replaced by et-et; thus the wishes of the minority were after all met in a decisive passage of the decree.[74]

On April 8, 1546 the decree was read out with the words "both . . . and." Trent did decide the relation of Scripture to tradition by rejecting Seripando's phrase and accepting "both . . . and" as a replacement for "partly . . . partly." The direction that debate at Trent was to follow on biblical study was determined by the implications of the "both . . . and" formula. Jedin is correct in saying that the thing itself of "partly . . . partly" was effectively decided at Trent. Trent frustrated the new biblical study which would utilize humanistic philology and evangelical terminology.[75]

---

72. Jedin, *A History of the Council of Trent,* II, p. 86.

73. Ibid., p. 87.

74. Ibid. See also H. Lennertz, "Scriptura et traditio in decreto 4. sessionis Concilii Tridentini," *Gregorianum,* 42 (1961):517–22. Lennertz states that the Council did not change its mind concerning the use of 'simili' and 'pari.' But Heiko Oberman finds it impossible on other grounds to accept "et . . . et," for it does not allow for tradition as a *viva vox euangelii.* The reasons advanced by Oberman are subject to further expansion. The "partim . . . partim" can be explained as a change of mind by the Council exactly because Bonucci and Nachianti received the support of Seripando and Pole.

75. See my "Biblical Humanism and Catholic Reform (1501-1541): Contarini, Pole and Giberti," *Concordia Theological Monthly,* 34 (1968):686–707. See also Louis B. Pascoe, S.J., "The Council of Trent and Bible Study: Humanism and Scripture " *Catholic Historical Review* 52 (1966-67):18–38.

To dismiss the Catholic biblical theologians at Trent as a minority party is to miss the point. Two Cardinal legates at Trent were representatives of evangelical biblical study in the pre-Tridentine period. Until a Conciliar decree countered their views on tradition and Scripture, their position was valid and truly Catholic. The linkage between tradition and works, Scripture and faith at Trent requires a closer scrutiny of Pole and Seripando during 1546.

Seripando and the Vulgate

Girolamo Seripando was born in Naples in 1492 or 1493. His early study showed him to be a student of rare promise. Lorenzo Giustiniani has put it nicely (allowing for the usual Italian hyperbole) that Seripando "had a grand love for study, an integrity in dress, sublimity of mind, a great concern, prudence in wisdom and was a pious Christian."[76] In 1510 Egidio of Viterbo, Augustinian General, took the young Seripando to Monte Cassino where they read Greek together.[77] Seripando learned Greek thoroughly and became an eminent theologian, learned in the sacred page and doctrines of the Fathers.[78] Seripando was a Platonist and humanist until the year 1530. Unfortunately, because of the lack of sources, we are not able to trace this humanistic or neo-Platonic emphasis except to Ficino and his Greek studies with Egidio.[79] The record after 1530 is far more promising, for Seripando cites an impressive array of ancient writers, notably Chrysostom and Eusebius. About 1530 all his study received a new perspective.[80]

---

76. Lorenzo Giustiniani, "Girolamo Seripando", *Biografa degli uomini illustri del Regno di Napoli orata de'loro rispettivi ritratti, compilata da diversi letterati nazionali, presso Nic Gervasi,* Napoli, 1813-1830, vol. I, p. 157.

77. Jedin, *Papal Legate at the Council of Trent,* p. 8.

78. Bart. Chioccarelli, *De Illustribus scriptoribus qui in civitate et regno Neapolis ab orbe condito ad annum usque MDCXXXVI floruerunt, ex officina Vic. Ursini,* Neapoli, 1780, Vol. I., p. 215, cols. i et ii.

79. John W. O'Malley, S.J., "Historical Thought and the Reform Crisis of the Early Sixteenth Century," *Theological Studies* 28 (1967):531–48.

80. Jedin, *Papal Legate at the Council of Trent,* p. 73. Also see Anselm Forster, *Gesetz und Evangelium bei Girolamo Seripando,* (Paderborn: Verlag Bonifacius-Druckerei, 1963.)

In 1539 Seripando evinced a remarkable interest in justification and biblical study. The exegetical nature of his work has been noted by Jedin:

Especially in his sermons to his brethern in the Order, he spoke of the justification of sinners, referring generally to the Pauline texts. . . . A large part of these beautiful addresses is no more than an exegesis of St. Paul. Even when explaining the duties of ecclesiastical superiors, he is guided by St. Paul. In spite of the exhausting demands of the visitation journey, he spent his free time in writing a commentary on the two epistles to the Corinthians and the Epistle to the Thessalonians. . . . He does not burden his commentary with many distinctions taken from systematic theology, but tries simply to explain Paul's meaning.[81]

Seripando was inspired to a new development of thought by reading St. Augustine's *De Spiritu et littera.*[82] Seripando gave two sermons in 1541 which revealed his new concept of justification and preoccupation with forgiveness. "He had begun with St. Thomas and Scotus, and now he had come to St. Augustine and St. Paul."[83] In his monastic visitations, Seripando utilized the literal meaning of Paul to protect and reform the Augustinian order. At Milan he "established a house of studies whose regent was to preach in Advent and lecture on the Scriptures during the year."[84] Seripando's eloquence as a preacher was well known.[85]

When Seripando heard the irenic speech of Cardinal Pole at Trent he recognized a kindred spirit. Their stand for the new humanistic exegesis and understanding of faith began with Pole's speech and was reflected

---

81. Jedin, *Papal Legate at the Council of Trent,* pp. 49–69.

82. Ibid., p. 88.

83. Ibid., p. 91.

84. Ibid., p. 141. While visiting Naples, Seripando delivered a brilliant sermon on II Corinthians 4:6, to which he attached a bill of reform promulgating a programme of study (Ibid., pp. 138–139).

85. Giov. Bernardino Tafuri, *Istoria degli Scrittori nati nel Regno di Napoli,* stamp. di Fel. Carlo Mosca: per gli Serverini, 1744-70, vol. 3, p. 198.

by Seripando's votes of 18 and 22 January 1546. He shared with Pole
the conviction that inner reform was first and most urgent.[86]

> Reformation is twofold, exterior and interior. Dogma pertains to
> interior reform which is stronger and requires the greatest atten-
> tion. After that the exterior reform will be more easily accom-
> plished—even without a council.[87]

On 22 January 1546 Seripando extolled the virtues of Cardinal Pole to
the Cardinal S. Crucis. " 'Today,' he said, 'truly I think the Holy Spirit
is among us.' "[88]

Subsequent statements of Seripando favor a distinction of degrees of
authority in Scripture. Two degrees should be recognized, said Seripando, one useful for doctrine and the rule of faith, the other for
doctrine and the rule of morality. The authority for faith rested upon
the inspiration of the Holy Spirit. Seripando's tract, *De libris sacrae
scripturae* places him within the Reforming circle of Pole.[89]

Seripando linked faith with Scripture (which has primary authority),
and tradition to Scripture (which must not be part of faith). This
condemnation of traditions which do not pertain to faith, even if in
Scripture, is astonishing. It suggests that Pole and Seripando's support
of the decree on justification was germane to the debates on Scripture
and tradition.[90] Seripando wanted the Council to recognize justification as the central doctrine in Scripture.

The Bishop of Aix (Aquensis) spoke for the approval of three texts
for doctrine in Greek, Latin, and Hebrew, and in his speech of 1 March
1546 he pointed out the differences between the Vulgate and existing
textual evidence.[91] In reply, Cardinal Cervini delivered a scathing in-

---

86. Jedin, *Papal Legate at the Council of Trent,* p. 263. Simultaneous discussion
of dogma and reform was begun; [Seripando] believed that the most serious
charges of the Protestants against the Church belonged to the field of dogma,
since they declared that in the Church the true gospel had been distorted."

87. *Concilium Tridentinum, Diarorum, Actorum, epistolarum, tractatuum noua
collectio,* ed. Soc. Goerresiana (Freiburg: Herder, 1901) V. 169, l. 318–21 (here-
after cited as *C.T.*)

88. *C.T.,* I. 23, l. 21.

89. *C.T.,* XII. 488, l. 24–29.

90. *C.T.,* XII. 518 l. 10–13.

91. *C.T.,* I. 500, l. 17–23.

dictment of those preachers ignorant of biblical languages whose allegations do not come from the font of the sacred books themselves, but are false and lead to error. In a speech the same day, Seripando too supported the attempt to purge the Vulgate.[92] Jedin comments:

> Seripando asked whether the sacred books should not be edited in a version corrected by comparison of the Vulgata with the Greek and Hebrew [texts]. It is clear that the true judge of Church and Scripture has been different in times.[93]

Cardinal Pole defended the toleration of many editions by the church in statements similar to those of Seripando.[94] The question was raised on 3 April, "whether the laity should be permitted to write biblical commentaries." Albert Pighius, a spokesman for the Catholic viewpoint, objected on the following grounds: "It is clear that to interpret contrary to the Church's sense is not permitted."[95] Pighius cited St. Jerome on the maximum distinction between clergy and laity.

In the vote on the Vulgate, Seripando voted, "Yes, that we may have the bible in three languages."[96] Pole voted his assent with the important qualification that there be editions of Scripture in Greek, Hebrew, and Latin for everyone's use in public reading, debate, and preaching.[97]

It is important to note that the Vulgate was left open to revision. "The ancient and wide-spread edition, tried by long and varied use in the Church" was declared "authentic," not "free from error."[98] Jedin comments:

> The course of the debate, whose main lines we have followed, leaves no room for any doubt that when it published this decree it was not the intention of the Council to restrict the study of the original languages of the Bible, still less to stop it. The production of a revised edition of the Vulgate is foreseen but no definite

---

92. *C.T.,* I. 506, l. 12–16.

93. *C.T.,* I. 507, l. 13–18.

94. *C.T.,* V. 65, l. 29–34.

95. *C.T.,* V. 64, l. 34–39.

96. *C.T.,* V. 66, l. 40.

97. *C.T.,* V. 66, l. 3–6.

98. Jedin, *A History of the Council of Trent,* II, p. 92.

statement is made about either the manner, or the place where the work should be done. The hotly controverted question of the translation of the Bible into the vernacular languages likewise remained unsolved. Holy Scripture may only be explained in the sense determined by the Church, its authentic interpreter, and confirmed by the unanimous consent of the Fathers. Not only editions and commentaries of the Bible, but all books with a theological content are subjected to a preventive censure by the Ordinary. The misuse of the word of God for profane and superstitious purposes is expressly condemned.[99]

One reason for objecting to the Vulgate decree advanced by Seripando was that the Latin texts lacked many passages useful for apologetics. Proverbs 8:35 and Deuteronomy 15:10 were arguments for freedom of the will. Proverbs 15:9 was crucial for the scholastic doctrine of faith formed by charity. "Sins are purged by mercy and by faith" was found in Latin translations of the Vulgate alone, out of all the other readings.[100]

Was it not possible that the Vulgate decree was passed with questions such these in the fore? Did not Pole and Seripando object to it so that the doctrine of *sola fide* might be defended from the Greek text and not excluded from an amplified Latin one? The apology of the Legates in letters of 24 and 26 April make it clear that the intent of decrees in the fourth session at Trent was to protect the dogmatic teaching office of the Church.[101]

From Seripando's suggestions and Pole's agreement one can re-examine the debates on justification of 1546. The "both . . . and" phrase left the question of tradition open; the Vulgate decree permitted appeal to tradition. Trent defeated Pole's and Seripando's support of the Hebrew and Greek texts. The third stage in the debates of 1546 would center on justification. The new hermeneutic based on literal exegesis and evangelical theology was thereby frustrated on 5 November 1546.[102]

---

99. Ibid., p. 92.

100. Jedin, *Papal Legate at the Council of Trent,* p. 299.

101. Ibid., pp. 96–97.

102. John W. O'Malley, S.J. has his doubts that Pole's views on justification were all that clearly expressed at Trent. See his review of Fenlon's *Heresy and Disobedience* in the *Catholic Historical Review* 61 (1975):104–105.

Recusant Response

English Catholics faced a particular difficulty. For, though the Council of Trent began in 1546 with Pole's address to the council fathers from *Ezekiel,* it ended in 1563 with the recusants in exile.

By 1550 the Catholic spokesman Stephen Gardiner, bishop of Winchester, had well answered Archbishop Thomas Cranmer's eucharistic writings,[103] but bitterness mounted as men on both sides abandoned sober biblical and patristic argument for invective and vilification. Thomas Harding took good measure of John Jewel in a restrained response to the 1562 *Apology of The Church of England,*[104] but John Rastell and Richard Smith minced few words in personal attacks on Jewel—and Peter Martyr.

Richard Martin's 1554 *Traictise* attacked clerical marriage which the Protestant John Poynet had defended in 1549.[105] Martin's *Traictise* identified lechery as the source of heresy. Poynet retorted in kind:

Ye know well enough that a nomber of your virgin preests may be, and be with you/both Sodomites/and whoremongers/ .... Master Doctor Martyn himself should be an heretique for kepinge Alice Lamme at the Christopher in Oxford. And Doctor Stories the lawyer also for kepinge madge Bowyer in Cramphole/& caetera.[106]

To borrow a phrase from Philip McNair, "Sin-in-the-head sprang from sin-in-the-bed." John Rastell, however, showed lightheartedness in his 1564 answer to Jewel's sermon preached at Paul's Cross (1560):

In reading, in using, in expownding of the scriptures, that no historie, prophecie, battell, name of person, place, or countrye, no hill, floud, field, nothing at all, shall escape us, but we will

---

103. Stephen Gardiner, *An Explicatiō/and assertion of the true Ca-/tholique fayth, touchying the moost ᵇlessed/Sacrament of the aulter with confuta-/cion of a booke written agaynst the/same* (Rouen: R. Caley, 1551).

104. Thomas Harding, *A Confutation of a Booke Intituled An Apologie of the Church of England* (Antwerp: John Laet, 1565).

105. Thomas Martin, *A Traictise declaryng, and plainly prouyng, that the pretended marriage of Priestes, and professed persones, is no marriage, but altogether unlawful,* ... (London: Robert Coly, 1554).

106. John Poynet, *An Apologie Fully Answeringe by Scriptures and Aunceāt Doctors a blasphemose Book.* ... (Strasburg: heirs of W. Köpfel?, 1555).

bring it unto some good sense, allegoricall, morall, or analogicall; we all knowe, that *Theologia mystica non est argumentis apta,* and that the sense misticall, ys not of sure strength in reasonyng: but our arke being sure, and the growndes of our religion being well setteled, and out of dawnger: for the rest, we may sing and plaie, and by ioyfull, and harpe upon the scripture.[107]

By 1582 English Catholics had produced their own New Testament at Rheims, and the Old Testament followed in 1609-1610 at Douai.[108] Quarrels over notes in the Geneva Bible (editions after 1560 introduced items such as Theodore Beza's predestinarian views) loom behind the scenes as do decades of controversy—from Stephen Gardiner to William Allen.[109]

The preface to the Rheims New Testament counterattackes the Protestant biblical versions from Tyndale onwards. The Rheims preface cites St. John Chrysostom's warning against private study and reading of Holy Writ:

[It is not] therfore (as some peruersely gather of his wordes) a thing absolutely needful for euery poore artificer to reade or studie Scriptures, nor any vvhit fauouring the presumptuous, curious, and contentious iangling and searching of Gods secretes, reproued by the foresaid fathers, much lesse approuing the excessive pride and madnes of these daies, vvhen euery man and vvoman is become not only a reader, but a teacher, controuler, and iudge of Doctors, Church, Scriptures and all: such as either contemne or easily passe ouer all the moral partes, good examples, and precepts of life . . . and only in a maner, occupie them selues in dogmatical, mystical, high and hidden secretes of Gods counsels, as of Predestination, reprobation, election . . . & other incomprehensible mysteries, *Languishing about questions* of onely faith, fiduce, nevv phrases and figures, *euer learning, but neuer comming to knovvledge,* reading and tossing in pride of vvite, conceite of their ovvne cunning, and vpon presumption of I

---

107. John Rastell, *A Confutation of a Sermon, pronoūced by M. Iuell, at Paules crosse . . .M.D.LX* (Antwerp: Aegidius Diest, 1564).

108. See accounts in F.F. Bruce, *The English Bible,* rev. ed. (London: Lutterworth Press, 1970), pp. 113–126 and A.C. Partridge, *English Biblical Translation* (London: Andre Deutsch, 1973), pp. 75–104.

109. See Martin Haile, *An Elizabethan Cardinal, William Allen* (London: Sir Isaac Bitman & Sons, Ltd., 1914).

can tell vvhat spirit, such books specially and Epistles, as S. Peter foretold that the vnlearned and instable vvould depraue to their ovvne damnation.[110]

The entire preface reflects the Protestant-Catholic controversy over vernacular biblical versions after Trent.

The Puritan scholar William Fulke (1538-1589), not to be outdone by the Catholic translator Gregory Martin, responded with his 1583 *Defense of the Sincere and true translations of the holie scriptures into the English tong,* reprinted twice in 1611 and again in 1633. Fulke intensified his attack on the Rheims New Testament through an edition in 1589. He answered Martin's preface point by point, and then arranged the Rheims version in parallel columns with the Bishops' Bible. Fulke reprinted the Rheim's notes with his own objections interspersed.

One interesting exchange occurred at Matthew 3:2, where Erasmus had earlier altered the Vulgate text away from "do penance." Martin had preserved the literal Vulgate, rendering verse two, "And saying, Doe penance: for the Kingdom of heaven is at hand." Fulke opposed this with the Bishops' Bible text, "And saying Repent ye: for the kingdom of heaven is at hand."[111] Martin, in the Rheims' note on Matthew 3:2 stated in part,

So is the Latine, word for work so readeth all antiquitie, namely S. Cyprian ep.52. often, and S. Augustine li 13. Confes.C.12. and it is a uery vsuall speach in the New Testament, specially in the preaching of S. Iohn Baptist,* Christ him selfe, and * the Apostles: to signifie perfect repentance, which hath not onely confession and amendment, but contrition or sorow for the offence, and painefull satisfaction: .... [112]

---

110. Gregory Martin, *The New Testament/of Jesus Christ, Trans-/lated Faithfully into English,/out of the authentical Latin . . . for the better vnder-/standing of the text, and specially for the discoverie of the/corrvptions of divers late translations, and for/cleering the controversies in religion, of these daies: . . .* (Rhemes: John Fogny, 1582), sig. aiiiir°-avv°.

111. William Fulke, *The/Text of the New/Testament of Jesvs/Christ, Translated ovt of/the vulgar latine by the Papistes of the traite-/rous Seminarie at Rhemes . . .* (London: Deputies of Christopher Barker, 1589), sig. D5r°.

112. Ibid., sig. D6r°.

Fulke answered that penance was an incorrect translation of both the Latin text and the Greek:

> And Beza doth iustly mislike your translation because in shewe of wordes . . . it fauoreth that blasphemous doctrine of satisfaction for sinne vnto the righteousnes of God, which was throughly performed by the sacrifice of Christes death.[113]

Further editions of Fulke in 1601, 1617, and 1633 gave the Rheims Bible—as well as the Fulke controversy—a wide circulation. Understandably, the translators of the 1611 Authorized Version dropped such marginal notes from the text.

---

113. Ibid., sig. D6r°.

Conclusion:
Word and Spirit

We have come full circle in our four chapters, from the humanist concern for Greek and Hebrew to the Catholic ambivalence about such biblical study at Trent and Rheims-Douai. George Williams of Harvard defines use of the Bible in the Radical Reformation under the rubric, "Word and Spirit."[1] It was Luther, after all, who complained that with the radicals all was "Geist, Geist, Geist." Gordon Rupp of Cambridge sees the hermeneutical problem as the contrast between the inner word and outer, the spirit of the writer and the letters chosen. The tensions at Wittenberg were matched by those at Zurich, Geneva, and Trent.

Magisterial Reformers did not ignore the Holy Spirit. Thus the Augsburg reformer Urbanus Rhegius in 1524 could say:

> The preacher brings God's word to our ears with the outward summons, but the finger of God writes it in the heart, and so the outward summons counts for nothing whether hearing, reading, writing, disputations, singing, until the Holy Ghost makes them active.[2]

The weakness of Radical appeal to the Spirit was the subordination of reason to emotion. Luther well said, "Do you not see how the devil is

---

1. George Williams, *The Radical Reformation* (Cambridge: Harvard University Press, 1962), pp. 816–32.

2. Gordon Rupp, "Word and Spirit In The Early Years of the Reformation," *Archiv für Reformationsgeschichte* 49 (1958):23.

the enemy of divine order? With the very words 'Spirit, spirit, spirit', he kicks away the very bridge by which the Spirit can come to you. . . ."[3] Again to the "Heavenly Prophets" Luther wrote:

> The man who would find God must seek Him in his Holy Word, he will not allow us to rely on anything else or hang our hearts on anything which is not Christ in His Word, be it as holy and full of Spirit as it may.[4]

In Geneva, Calvin clashed with Castellio, who appealed to Christ in His Word. According to Castellio, the Bible was a library in which God and man might meet.[5] Castellio wanted the Song of Solomon removed from that library. The ministers of Geneva resisted such a weeding of the canon:

> Castellio said that it was a lascivious and obscene poem in which Solomon described his indecent amours. . . . As for the book we contended that it was an epithalamium not unlike Psalm 45.[6]

More serious was the exegetical crusade mounted by the Socinians, who did not separate inner meaning from outer text, nor did they reduce the canon of scripture. Within the Radical Reformation emerged their concern for the humanity of Jesus as found in Faustus Socinus' treatise, *De Jesu Christo Servatore* (1578). These subtle Italians accused Rome of teaching "three Gods and one wife," and instead claimed that man should have "one God and three wives."[7] Professor Van Den Brink observes that the Reformation taught the Church to find new strength in the Bible. In spite of quarrels, he says, the Bible reformed the church and will go on doing so as long as the church's pilgrimage lasts.[8]

---

3. Ibid., p. 24.

4. Ibid., p. 25.

5. Williams, *Radical Reformation*, pp. 817–18.

6. Roland Bainton, "The Bible in the Age of the Reformation," in *The Cambridge History of the Bible*, p. 8.

7. Philip McNair, "Ochino's Apology: Three Gods or Three Wives?" *History* 60 (1975):353–73.

8. J. N. Bakhuizen Van Den Brink, "Bible and Biblical Theology in the Early Reformation," *Scottish Journal of Theology* 15 (1962):65. See details of the 1976 sessions on sixteenth century exegesis reported by Bernard Roussel, "Le premier colloque international d'histoire de l'exégèse biblique au XVIe siecle. Genève 29.9–1.10. 1976, *"Bibliothèque D'Humanisme Et Renaissance* 39 (1977):167–71.

We began our survey of the Bible in the Reformation with the Humanist critique of the Vulgate, the Latin Bible of the church for twelve hundred years. Valla's linguistic approach was used to break down confidence in the text and Protestant reliance on its sole authority.[9] Next we glanced at Wittenberg, where Martin Luther's canonical skepticism was revealed. Luther's skepticism still finds adherents today, as evidenced by the Kittel *Theological Word Book of the New Testament.* Rudolf Bultmann's article on faith, for example, contains accents of the sixteenth-century debate over *sola fide.*

We next turned to Reformed certainty about biblical passages, which led Geneva to burn Servetus and Zurich to drown Anabaptists. Theodore Beza developed a scheme whereby political resistance could be supported in spite of Romans 13:1-3.[10] John Ponet's political treatise on rebellion chose Acts 5:39 to support tyrannicide (since Peter said, "We must obey God rather than men"). Religious wars supported by this kind of exegesis of Scripture swept over France.

Finally, we glanced at the Catholic Pauline renaissance before and after the Inquisition of 1542 crushed such confidence in Scripture. The electricity of those early decades turned to suspicion and strife as ecclesiastical authorities jealously guarded their control over scriptural interpretation and so battled over the gospel.

Professor Ebeling holds that the history of the church is best seen in its interpretation of Scripture.[11] As custodian of the canon certain lessons must come home to the body of Christ. First of all, it is clear that sixteenth-century biblical study divided Europe and the New World into confessional jungles. A second lesson emerges from King Edward VI. He granted letters patent to the Strangers Churches in London, who get their name from Ephesians 2:19, which reads: "No more are you strangers and sojurners, but . . . fellow-citizens with the saints

9. Richard Popkin, "The Intellectual Crisis of the Reformation," in his *History of Scepticism from Erasmus to Descartes* (Assen: Van Gorcum & Co., 1964), pp. 1–16.

10. Robert Kingdon, "The First Expression of Theodore Beza's Political Ideas," *Archiv für Reformationsgeschichte* 46 (1955):88–99.

11. B. Roussel, "Histoire de L'Eglise et Histoire de L'Exégèse au XVIe siecle," *Bibliotheque D'Humanisme et Renaissance* 37 (1975):181–92. Also see account of colloquium to be published in 1978.

and the household of God." It was appropriate that those followers of Christ—Himself a stranger and exile while on earth—should cling to the portable Ark rather than to the stationary Temple.

We visited the violence of Catholic Inquisition and Protestant persecution. Dürer's Four Apostles set the scene for the entire century as the dread horsemen of the Apocalypse thundered through those desperate decades. Yet always there seemed to be another rider at their head flashing His sword—the Lamb of God, going forth conquering and to conquer.

Use of the Bible in the Reformation was a matter of life and death. As William Tyndale said:

> Scripture is the light and life of God's elect, and that mighty power wherewith God createth them and shapeth them after the similitude, likeness and very fashion of Christ. . . . Therefore are they faithful servants of Christ . . . which have given themselves up into the hand of God, and put themselves in jeopardy of all persecution, their very life despised, and have translated the scripture purely and with good conscience. . . .[12]

Commentary, confession, and controversy show how lively and enlightened the sixteenth century church became as it wrestled like Jacob of old. Though the church emerged from that century-long struggle crippled by controversy and religious wars, many like William Tyndale enjoyed the blessing of God on their labors. Scripture was the mighty power whereby God shaped His faithful servants after the very fashion of Christ.

---

12. William Tyndale, *The Exposition of the Fyrste Epistle of Seynt Jhon* (1531), in T.H.L. Parker, *English Reformers* (Philadelphia: Westminster Press, 1966), p. 105.

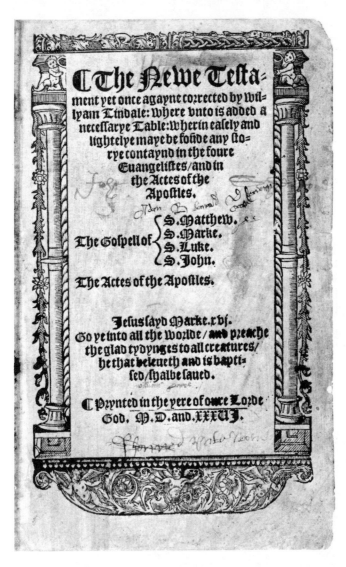

One of three distinct quarto editions of the Tyndale New Testament, all printed in 1536. This is the first and "Mole" edition, named for the engraving of St. Paul which is prefixed to the eleven epistles. In this edition Paul's foot rests on a stone bearing a figure of a mole. In the other two the stone is blank or marked with the engraver's monogram, A.K.B.

Index of Names